CAPTAIN AMERICA vs IRON man

Freedom, Security, Psychology

Edited by
TRAVIS LANGLEY, PHD

STERLING
New York

STERLING
New York

An Imprint of Sterling Publishing Co., Inc.
1166 Avenue of the Americas
New York, NY 10036

Text © 2016 by Travis Langley

ISBN 978-1-4549-1712-0

Distributed in Canada by Sterling Publishing
c/o Canadian Manda Group, 664 Annette Street
Toronto, Ontario, Canada M6S 2C8
Distributed in the United Kingdom by GMC Distribution Services
Castle Place, 166 High Street, Lewes, East Sussex, England BN7 1XU
Distributed in Australia by Capricorn Link (Australia) Pty. Ltd.
P.O. Box 704, Windsor, NSW 2756, Australia

For information about custom editions, special sales, and premium and corporate purchases,
please contact Sterling Special Sales at 800-805-5489 or specialsales@sterlingpublishing.com.

Manufactured in Canada

2 4 6 8 10 9 7 5 3 1

www.sterlingpublishing.com

Picture credits – see page 168

To Danny Fingeroth
who made me think, "I want to
write this kind of book."

CONTENTS

III. IDEALS

OUR HEROES

Long before I knew Danny Fingeroth, his 2004 book *Superman on the Couch: What Superheroes Really Tell Us about Ourselves and Our Society* made me think, "I want to write this kind of book." His observation that "it has been decades since psychiatry or psychology has taken a look at such questions about superheroes"[1] stayed with me when I later attended San Diego Comic-Con for the first time. There, I met comics scholars through the Comics Arts Conference (Comic-Con's academic conference-within-the-con), watched people circulate throughout the con environment, which celebrated interests they might not get to share in other settings in their lives, and knew I needed to become part of it all. I wanted to explore "such questions" as Danny had mentioned. The esteemed Mr. Fingeroth has been a comic book writer, Spider-Man group editor, book author, panel organizer, educator, and friend. His works include *The Stan Lee Universe*[2] and *Disguised as Clark Kent: Jews, Comics, and the Creation of the Superhero,*[3] the latter of which (like this book) features a foreword by Stan "the Man."

For my Comics Arts Conference (CAC) presentation at that particular Comic-Con, I analyzed Marvel Comics' *Civil War* storyline.[4] Years after the original 2006–2007 comic book storyline began, we're still talking about it now. I therefore thank my fellow CAC organizers Peter Coogan, Randy Duncan, and Kathleen McClancy, along with my son Nicholas because I attended the conference to see him speak as a member of Matthew Smith's CAC panel on con culture. Through CAC and other venues, scholars like Arlen Schumer work hard to help inform the masses about creators such as Joe Simon and Jack Kirby, whose names should be widely known. Because I met most of this book's contributors through Comic-Con, *Captain America vs. Iron Man* could never have come together this way without everyone who ever played parts in getting us to San Diego that first time. We therefore thank San Diego Comic-Con International's organizers (Eddie Ibrahim, Sue Lord, Adam Neese, Gary Sassaman, and company) who provide the Comics Arts Conferences programming time, facilities, and support.

Many different conventions help this book's writers meet each other, make plans, and share thoughts. I must always thank Wizard World programming director Christopher Jansen and others who keep their cons going across the land. My first one-on-one conversation with Stan Lee took place at Wizard World Philadelphia Comic Con, courtesy of Clare Kramer the Buffy-slayer. After Stan told me, "You should teach Stan Lee University," I put together a course titled *Stan Lee Heroes*, using the marvels he and his collaborators created in order to teach real psychology. At Wizard World New Orleans Comic Con, Stan answered my students' questions after *Stan Lee's Who Wants to Be a Superhero?* champion Jarrett Crippen helped pick the best of their questions. Gates McFadden (*Star Trek: The Next Generation*) once stopped by my Wizard World table and struck up a conversation comparing Batman and Iron Man, making particular note of Tony Stark's "narcissistic wound" and ultimately inspiring me to add this book's features about id, ego, and superego.

Comics pros who've joined us on panels to discuss this book's featured heroes include Paul Benjamin, Victor Dandridge, Steve Englehart, Tania Del Rio, Devin Grayson, Molly Mahan, Bryan Q. Miller, Jim Salicrup, J. J. Sedelmaier, Gail Simone, Nicky Wheeler-Nicholson, Denny O'Neil, David Uslan, Marguerite Van Cook, Len Wein, and Marv Wolfman. Professionals of other kinds on those panels have included Eric Bailey, NYPD Sgt. Mike Bruen, Abby Dark Star, Kieran Dickson, Andrea Letamendi, Jessica Merizan, Robert O'Nale, Robin Rosenberg, Derek Royal, Aaron Sagers, David Uslan, and Xena Zeit-Geist. My students continually help me flesh out ideas about these characters, and while there are too many students to name, I will point out Mitchell Cullins, Christine Dickson, Brianna George, Ben Graves, Mitchell Green, Brian Lott, Samantha Proffit, and Sean Shuttleworth among those who went the extra mile to make relevant conference presentations.

Our university's Comics Arts Club, Legion of Nerds; students minoring in comics studies; others taking our nerdy classes; and alumni who formed the Comic Arts Council are, themselves, our comics studies' driving power. The students, other faculty members who teach comics studies courses, and I are truly fortunate to teach at a university where administrators like President Glen Jones, Provost Steve Adkison, and Dean John Hardee have encouraged creative ways of teaching. My fellow psychology faculty members show great support: Rafael Bejarano, Emilie Beltzer, Rebecca Langley, Paul Williamson, and our chair, Aneeq Ahmad. I must thank now-retired chair Todd Wiebers for saying that if Stan Lee himself suggested I teach a course on Lee's co-creations, then I should go right ahead. Librarian Lea Ann Alexander and the Huie Library staff maintain Henderson State University's impressive graphic novel reading room. Linda Mooney, Millie Bowden, and other fine Henderson State University staff members help us all make sure things can get done. Our faculty writers group (Angela Boswell, Matthew Bowman, Vernon Miles, Suzanne Tartamella, Michael Taylor) help me build, rebuild, and fine tune the literary machine.

Sterling Publishing editor Connie Santisteban got me started on this project and graciously passed the editing torch to Kate Zimmerman. Kalista Johnston, Marilyn Kretzer, Sari Lampert, Blanca Oliviery, Lauren Tambini, and other Sterling superheroes go above and beyond the call of duty to help us complete and promote these projects. Mara Whiteside Wood and Jenna Busch have been conscientious editorial assistants on this volume, both ready to take on one strange new task after another. Jenna previously worked for Stan Lee, co-hosting "Cocktails with Stan" on YouTube, and they've remained close. She discussed this book with him, and the thoughts he shared then became the basis for his foreword. We thank POW! Entertainment's Yuka Kobayashi for setting that up, and we certainly thank the man born Stanley Lieber for the foreword itself. Also worthy of mention are Jeff Caudle, Michael French, Erica Ash Lemons, Greg Lemons, John McManus, Louis Monoyudis, Patrick Murphy, Chris Murrin, Robert O'Nale, Greg Walker, Tiffany Pitcock, Justin Poole, Kevin Michael Scott, Ryan L. Sittler, photographers Lawrence Brenner and Bill Ostroff, and family-not-by-blood Renee Couey, Marko Head, and Katrina Hill.

Joe Simon and Jack Kirby created Captain America. Stan Lee later conceived Iron Man, which he created with Larry Lieber, Don Heck, and again Jack Kirby. Hundreds upon hundreds of other storytellers made valuable contributions over the years, like Steve Englehart who pitted Captain America against an American president, David Micheline who turned Iron Man into an alcoholic, and Dennis O'Neal who made Tony Stark fall off the wagon. Did Allen Bellman, Steve Epting, Mike Zeck, or someone else pencil the best post-Kirby Captain America? Did Bob Layton draw the definitive Iron Man? (You'd have to visit my office to see Layton's original illustration of Iron Man playing golf.) By turning Captain America and Iron Man from long-time allies into opponents leading superhero armies, writers Mark Millar and Brian Michael Bendis created the conflict that led us to write this book. Even so, the issue at the heart of their fight—superheroes' freedom versus national or world security—has roots that stretch back to the origins of both characters within the comics, to theories of psychologist Erich Fromm, and to struggles that have continued since before known human history began.

References

Fingeroth, D. (2004). *Superman on the couch: What superheroes really tell us about ourselves and our society.* New York, NY: Continuum.

Fingeroth, D. (2007). *Disguised as Clark Kent: Jews, comics, and the creation of the superhero.* New York, NY: Bloomsbury Academic.

Fingeroth, D. (2011). *The Stan Lee universe.* Raleigh, NC: TwoMorrows.

Langley, T. (2007, July). *Freedom versus security: The basic human dilemma from 9/11 to Marvel's Civil War.* Comics Arts Conference. Comic-Con International, San Diego, CA.

Langley, T. (2009). Freedom versus security: The basic human dilemma from 9/11 to Marvel's Civil War. *International Journal of Comic Art, 11*(1), 426–435.

Langley, T. (2015). Freedom versus security: The basic human dilemma from 9/11 to Marvel's Civil War. In K. M. Scott (Ed.), *Marvel Comics' Civil War and the age of terror: Critical essays on the comic saga* (pp. 69–76). Jefferson, NC: McFarland.

Notes

1. Fingeroth (2004), p. 22.
2. Fingeroth (2011).
3. Fingeroth (2007).
4. Langley (2007, 2009, 2015).

CAPTAIN AMERICA

Creators: Joe Simon & Jack Kirby.
Debut: *Captain America Comics* #1 (1941, March). "Meet Captain America." Script: Joe Simon. Art: Jack Kirby & Al Liederman.
Revival: *The Avengers* #4 (1964, March). "Captain America Joins the Avengers!" Script: Stan Lee. Art: Jack Kirby & George Roussos.
First Theatrical Appearance: *Captain America* (1944 movie serial). Republic Pictures.

IRON MAN

Creators: Stan Lee, Larry Lieber, Don Heck, & Jack Kirby.
Debut: *Tales of Suspense* #39 (1963, March). "Iron Man is Born!" Script: Stan Lee. Art: Jack Kirby & Don Heck.
First Theatrical Appearance: *Iron Man* (2008 motion picture). Marvel Studios, Fairview Entertainment.

THE PUBLISHER: IT'S ALL MARVEL

Captain America, Iron Man, and related Marvel Universe characters originate in publications from Marvel Comics. The company has undergone several name changes during its history.

Timely Publications: founded in 1939, soon renamed **Timely Comics**.
Atlas Comics: new company name starting in 1951.
Marvel Comics: rebranded in summer 1961. Official company name has been **Marvel Publishing**, **Marvel Comics Group**, and **Marvel Worldwide**.
Parent company: Marvel Enterprises, then **Marvel Entertainment** (part of **The Walt Disney Company** as of 2009).
Location: New York, NY.

Because most comics cited herein were published by Timely/Atlas/Marvel, references will identify a comic book's publisher only for the few instances in which an outside company such as DC published the work.

THE HEAD! THE HEART! THE HEROES!

STAN LEE

I've never studied psychology officially, but all around us, everything in the world involves psychology. The way you behave with other people. The image you want to leave of yourself with other people. Your association with other people. Everything you say, everything you do is linked to psychology. That's what I wanted to bring to our superheroes.

Steve Rogers wasn't the first superhero dressed in the American flag, but he became the most popular. I think it was because he was drawn so well by Jack Kirby and because

Left: Jenna Busch; right: Stan Lee.

Joe Simon's stories were really very exciting in the early days. Captain America had heart. Some people call Iron Man the brains of the Avengers and Captain America the heart, and I think that comes really close to it. After we brought Captain America back and then he led the Avengers for the first time, the entire team was made up of former criminals like the Scarlet Witch and Quicksilver. Cap is a big believer in second chances. Anybody would be a believer in that if they're logical and if they have the slightest bit of sympathy for other people. Anybody can make a mistake. And if you can find somebody who's made a mistake and you can put them on the right track, what a wonderful thing that is to do.

Captain America was the quintessential World War II hero and then Iron Man came out of a different war with a different generation. I wanted to have fun with Iron Man. I took all the things the hippies hated and I let Iron Man represent them. He was a guy who made munitions. He helped the nation's war effort. He was a billionaire, a ladies man. I thought, it will be fun to see if I can make him popular. Funny thing is, he became incredibly popular with female readers. We had more fan mail from females for Iron Man than any other character. I think the thing that really makes Tony Stark so appealing is that he is a little bit of an egomaniac. He's conceited, but he has every reason to be conceited. I mean, here's a guy who's handsome, he's a billionaire, he's a fighter, he's an inventor, and he's also got a weak heart. You can't get a more interesting guy than that. If I were creating a character now, it would probably be closer to Iron Man. Captain America is wonderful, but he's just such a perfect human being. I think you can have more fun with people who have a little more imperfection. That's Marvel in a nutshell!

In *Civil War*, these heroes tussle over whether superheroes should register with the government. I don't see anything wrong with registering. If that would make life easier and make people happier, it's fine with me. If the heroes want to do it and if the government wants them to do it, why not? Of course, Captain America's experience against enemies like Hydra differs from Iron Man's—enemies who want to infiltrate the government and take over S.H.I.E.L.D. When we created Hydra, I wanted them to be a mysterious group who, if you kill one, a hundred others appear. You can't get rid of them. In fact, I even wrote a saying that they had: "Hail, Hydra! Immortal Hydra! We shall never be destroyed! Cut off a limb, and two more shall take its place! We serve none but the Master—as the world shall soon serve us! Hail Hydra!" They are sort of like ISIS today. There are so many of them. And if you kill a few, it doesn't mean anything. There are a lot more. Captain America and Iron Man oppose them and all the other villains because they're the good guys and in fiction, the good guys keep on fighting as long as there's something to fight for. And thanks to groups like Hydra, there will always be something to fight for, and that always gives us great stories to write.

Who's in the right—Captain America, the self-sacrificing hero, or Iron Man, the war profiteer? They're both right. I think it's possible to be all kinds of different people with different personalities and you can all be right. The point is, both of them do good things. Both of them are good to other people and they make the world a better place in their own way. Which one I root for depends how you position them in the story. There are places where Captain America can shine and there are places where you just have to have Iron Man. As a writer, you put the character in the right place at the right time and where the reader would appreciate him the most.

I think that anybody reading these stories about these characters should just sit back and expect to be amazed and astonished by *Captain America vs. Iron Man*, and hopefully to see things that they hadn't expected to see. Things that they'll enjoy because they're so provocative.

Excelsior!

Left: Travis Langley; right: Stan Lee.

THE SHIELD, THE ARMOR, AND THE BASIC HUMAN DILEMMA

TRAVIS LANGLEY

The first time I chatted with Stan Lee, we discussed his intuitive psychology. He and his co-creators brought human depth to Marvel superheroes at a time when other comic book superheroes were often a bit flat. His heroes bickered among themselves, worried about paying bills, sometimes had health problems, and felt conflicted about their actions. Ego and angst often drove them, and they would call one another on those very things.

Well, that's what we talked about after getting past the fact that I'd written a book about a character not of his creation,[1] one with such complexity that *The Avengers* filmmaker Joss Whedon once called him a "Marvel character in the DC universe."[2]

> **Stan:** Batman? Why would you want to write a book about him?
> **Travis:** He's more screwed up than your characters.
> **Stan:** This man is a genius![3]

A more thorough answer to Stan's question might, in part, also apply to why we analyze Captain America and Iron Man: simply because they share some of the same qualities that make that Dark Knight so popular. They're human. Not only do they start off fully human in their origin stories, they remain human, and it shows. Even though each of them excels in areas of intellect, physical skill, and sheer determination, neither has the kind of ability people typically think of as a superpower. Their talents are more believable than shape shifting, mind reading, turning invisible, or controlling the weather. We can relate to them and their motives. Although every superhero becomes a hero because of his or her psychology, most are super for fantastic reasons beyond their control. A few, though, choose to become super, to turn themselves into larger-than-life figures while remaining fully human. Not only does making a choice to do the right thing look more heroic, it feels more altruistic to the hero as well and reinforces the heroism and sense of capability in that individual's nature.[4] Steve Rogers could lose the muscle the Super-Soldier project added to his frame, and Tony Stark could lose access to his money and fancy toys, yet they'll both still have the kinds of minds and passion that turned them into the heroes in the first place.[5] Each would persist. Because they seem more intrinsically heroic, they are therefore figures the other heroes will more readily follow into any situation.

Unfortunately for them, the humanity Stan and company invested in them can also put them at odds.

> *"Genuine tragedies in the world are not conflicts between*
> *right and wrong. They are conflicts between two rights."*
> —attributed to philosopher Georg Wilhelm Friedrich Hegel[6]

On the large scale, the story told in *Civil War* #1–7 and related Marvel publications depicts armies of superheroes fighting over a congressional act that requires all superhumans to register their abilities and identities with the federal government, undergo training, and serve the government whether they like it or not. It was not the first story to look at what might happen if the government tries to regulate superheroes. Comic books and graphic novels (e.g., *Kingdom Come; Watchmen*), motion pictures (*The Return of Captain Invincible; The Incredibles*), and television programs (*Smallville*) had all visited that terrain. *Civil War* explored it across a comic book company's entire mainstream line, altering character relationships and affecting stories for years to come in a way no other crossover event had previously achieved. Across these many stories, characters who become registration supporters typically hold that registering is the responsible thing to do and that no one should place himself or herself above the law. Opponents of registration argue instead that such regulation violates civil liberties, with some comparing it to segregation or slavery, and insist that no government is secure enough. A government that cannot protect its own secrets therefore cannot protect superheroes and their loved ones from the supervillains they spend their lives fighting.

On the most personal level, though, it's a fight between two men. From when they each debut, Steve Rogers (Captain America) fights for freedom and Tony Stark (Iron Man) develops weapons for national security.[7] Neither position is out of character. They have often fallen on opposite sides of what Erich Fromm called "the basic human dilemma": freedom versus security.[8] No problem has put them at such odds over it before.

Sociologist-turned-psychologist Erich Fromm fled his homeland when the Nazis rose to power. He tried to make sense of why members of the German population, suffering from the Great Depression, gave up so many of their liberties for seeming security under a dictatorial regime. He concluded that people feel competing desires for both freedom and security. Fear can drive people to relinquish freedom to feel safe and secure, and yet oppression can drive them to tear down the

A TALE OF TWO EGOS

Science, history, and hindsight show us that as a conflict escalates, participants on both sides can lose sight of why it began. It grows increasingly personal, particularly for the leaders. Whoever leads the losing side, if anyone wins at all, can be seen as the losing general, manager, or coach. The comic book version of *Civil War* ends when one leader surrenders for the sake of protecting others the conflict might harm, when he gives up an apparent victory rather than risk harming others, when he values peace over the point he has been trying to make and even above his own self-esteem.

Civil War is not the first fight between Captain America and Iron Man. Superheroes have a long history of getting into skirmishes with one another over their egos or as a result of misunderstandings. A few months after the Avengers thaw out Captain America and welcome him to the team, a villain impersonates Captain America and tricks Iron Man into attacking Cap.[9] After they finally clear things up, Iron Man sits berating himself as he mulls over how easily the villain fooled him: "Sometimes I grow overconfident in my super-powered armor!"

Assessing the harm of one's own overconfidence indicates a degree of personal insight that suggests that the person does *not* have the condition known as *narcissistic personality disorder*.[10] Even though Tony Stark's ego is huge and he does possess a number of narcissistic qualities, he has achievements commensurate with his self-concept and tries to keep his ego in check throughout his character arc.

system in order to breathe free. The conflict can cycle back and forth without end. Comic book writers Brian Michael Bendis and Mark Millar conceived Marvel's *Civil War* in the wake of 9/11, when the USA PATRIOT Act limited liberties and broadened the government's abilities. Whether they knew it or not, they pitted hero against hero in a superpowered illustration of what Fromm called the basic human dilemma: the clash between freedom and security.[11]

This book's contributors compare and contrast these heroes' psyches in a variety of ways. It's not all about one climactic confrontation between characters. We examine stories spun over the course of decades, the better part of a century, in looking at the superheroes and how their experiences reflect the psychology of real human beings. Captain America and Iron Man emerge as different types of leaders for many reasons relating to their personalities, life experiences, and motivations, and these stories do much more than entertain us. They speak to us as occupants of a world where we regularly must consider personalities, life experiences, and motivations of many kinds. Within these pages, our superteam of psychologists and therapists, sometimes joined by other experts, share their musings as both professionals and fans.

We are particularly grateful to Stan "the Man" Lee for joining us. He created Iron Man together with Larry Lieber, Don Heck, and Jack Kirby. Lee and Kirby soon assembled the Avengers and then brought Captain America into the team. By killing off his boy sidekick Bucky and making Cap a man out of his time, they added poignancy and additional depth to the character Kirby had co-created with Joe Simon long before. We thank them all for giving us these heroes, and we thank Stan in particular for this book's marvelous foreword.

During that first conversation of ours, the master of marvels also told me, "You should teach Stan Lee University." So I soon taught a class using heroes Lee co-created to illustrate principles of psychology, and Stan answered my students' questions. With *Captain America vs. Iron Man: Freedom, Security, Psychology,* we're taking that a bit further.

And you don't have to choose sides.

> *"The more we face our own conflicts and seek out our own solutions, the more inner freedom and strength we will gain."*
> —psychoanalyst Karen Horney[12]

> *"The harder the conflict, the more glorious the triumph."*
> —author Thomas Paine[13]

Comic Book References

Captain America Comics #1 (1941). "Meet Captain America." Script: J. Simon. Art: J. Kirby & A. Liederman.

Captain America #300 (1984). Script: J. M. DeMatteis. Art: P. Neary & D. Janke.

Civil War #1–7 (2006–2007). Script: M. Millar. Art: S. McNiven, D. Vines, J. Dell, & T. Townsend.

Kingdom Come #1–4 (1996). Script: M. Waid. Art: A. Ross. (DC Comics.)

Tales of Suspense #39 (1963, March). "Iron Man Is Born!" Script: S. Lee. Art: J. Kirby & D. Heck.

Tales of Suspense #58 (1964). "In Mortal Combat with Captain America!" Script: S. Lee. Art: D. Heck, J. Kirby, & D. Ayers.

Watchmen #1–13 (1986–1987). Scripts: A. Moore. Art: D. Gibbons. (DC Comics.)

Other References

Adler, J. (2013). *Soulmates from the pages of history.* New York, NY: Algora.

American Psychiatric Association (2013). *Diagnostic and statistical manual of mental disorders* (DSM-5). Washington, DC: American Psychiatric Association.

Ellithorpe, M. E., Ewoldsen, D. R., & Oliver, M. B. (2015). Elevation (sometimes) increases altruism: Choice and number of outcomes in elevating media effects. *Psychology of Popular Media Culture, 43,*(3), 236–250.

Evry, M. (2013, May 30). *Joss Whedon Talks Quicksilver, Firefly, and . . . Batman???* Super Hero Hype: http://www.superherohype.com/news/177205-joss-whedon-talks-quicksilver-firefly-and-batman.

Flynn, K., & Lavoie, R. (2010). *Our little secret.* New York, NY: Penguin.

Fromm, E. (1941). *Escape from freedom.* New York, NY: Rinehart.

Fromm, E. (1955). *The sane society.* New York, NY: Rinehart.

Halvorsen, R. E. (2009). An exploitation of tragedy. In C. Hamilton, O. Neumaier, G. Schweiger, & C. Sedmak (Eds.), *Facing tragedies* (pp. 59–66). New Brunswick, NJ: Transaction.

Harvey, J. H., & Harris, B. (1975). Determinants of perceived choice and the relationship between perceived choice and expectancy about feelings of internal control. *Journal of Personality and Social Psychology, 31*(1), 101–106.

Horney, K. (1945). *Our inner conflicts: A constructive theory of neurosis.* Oxford, UK: Routledge.

Jellison, J. M., & Harvey, J. M. (1973). Determinants of perceived choice and the relationship between perceived choice and perceived competence. *Journal of Personality and Social Psychology, 28*(3), 376–382.

Kanfer, F. H., & Grimm, L. G. (1978). Freedom of choice and behavioral change. *Journal of Consulting and Clinical Psychology, 46*(5), 873–878.

Langley, T. (2007, July). *Freedom versus security: The basic human dilemma from 9/11 to Marvel's Civil War.* Comics Arts Conference. Comic-Con International, San Diego, CA.

Langley, T. (2009). Freedom versus security: The basic human dilemma from 9/11 to Marvel's Civil War. *International Journal of Comic Art, 11*(1), 426–435.

Langley, T. (2012). *Batman and psychology: A dark and stormy knight.* New York, NY: Wiley.

Langley, T. (2015). Freedom versus security: The basic human dilemma from 9/11 to Marvel's *Civil War.* In K. M. Scott (Ed.), *Marvel Comics' Civil War and the age of terror: Critical essays on the comic saga* (pp. 69–76). Jefferson, NC: McFarland.

Ma, J., Wang, S., & Hao, W. (2012). Does cultural similarity matter? Extending the animosity model from a new perspective. *Journal of Consumer Marketing, 29*(5), 319–332.

McCarthy, P. R., & Rogers, T. (1982). Effects of gain versus loss of reward on actual and perceived altruism. *Psychological Reports, 51*(1), 319–322.

Memmott, R. (2004). *The divine paradox.* Salt Lake City, UT: Compass.

Paine, T. (1776). *The American crisis,* pamphlet no. 1. Philadelphia, PA: Styner & Cist.

Notes

1. Langley (2012).
2. Evry (2013).
3. Personal communication (2012, June 2).
4. Ellithorpe et al. (2015); Harvey & Harris (1975); Jellison & Harvey (1973); Kanfer & Grimm (1978); McCarthy & Rogers (1982).
5. *Captain America* #300 (1984); *Iron Man 3* (2013 motion picture).
6. Most sources attribute this to Hegel (e.g., Adler, 2013, p. 109; Memmott, 2004, p. 85) while a few instead credit playwright Friedrich Christian Hebbel (e.g., Flynn & Lavoie, 2010, part 4; Halvorsen, p. 66). Our search of all their published works finds no such quote, but that could be a matter of translation.
7. *Captain America Comics* #1 (1941); *Tales of Suspense* #39 (1963).
8. Fromm (1941, 1955).
9. *Tales of Suspense* #58 (1964).
10. American Psychiatric Association (2013).
11. Langley (2007, 2009, 2015).
12. Horney (1945), p. 47.
13. Paine (1776).

PART ONE

ORIGINS

An origin story opens in the middle, after personality has spent years taking shape, after awareness of things people call good and evil has long since begun to bloom. One classic theory in psychology posits that morality develops in stages. The part that stays with us may have less to do with who's right or wrong and more to do with the reasoning that goes into making moral choices in the first place.

CHAPTER ONE

MORAL DECISIONS IN MARVEL'S *CIVIL WAR*: STAGES OF HERO DEVELOPMENT

MARA WOOD

"A moral principle is an obligatory or ideal rule of choice between legitimate alternatives, rather than a concrete prescription of action."
—developmental psychologist Lawrence Kohlberg[1]

". . . the best part about being an Avenger? Having Captain America around you all the time. He just— the guy just brings out the absolute best in people. You want to be good when he's around."
—Clint Barton (Hawkeye)[2]

Good people can get into a fight. In the comic books, after working together for years, Captain America and Iron Man wing up, leading opposing sides in a superhero fight over a law that requires all superhumans to register with the government,

trust the system to protect their secret identities, receive training, and work in law enforcement whether they want to or
not. Everyone in a dispute may be a bit wrong and a bit right
for a variety of reason. One classic theory on stages of moral
development may help us understand the perspectives of the
characters involved in Marvel's *Civil War* storyline or any real
dispute as well as the rationale for decisions made and actions
taken. Different individuals can demonstrate all six stages
of moral development on both sides of the issue. As Doctor
Strange comments, "There is no right or wrong in this debate.
It is simply a matter of perspective. . . ."[3]

Stages of Moral Development

At any specific moment, we must be able to make decisions
about what we consider right and wrong. These decisions are
often unique to the decision-maker. Consider the following
moral dilemma:

> A woman had a special kind of cancer that could be
> cured by a new drug discovered by a druggist nearby.
> However, the druggist was charging ten times what
> the drug cost him to make. The woman's husband
> could not afford the drug, and the druggist refused to
> alter his price. The husband stole the drug. Should he
> have done that?

Lawrence Kohlberg's studies of morality and moral development[4] in children and adolescents hinged on situations like the
one involving the husband and the druggist.[5] He presented boys
with this scenario and others with equally ambiguous answers.

It was not the answer per se that intrigued Kohlberg but the reasoning behind the boys' decisions. The "right" answer can be debated, but the path to the decision allows for insight into the moral development of the boy.

From his initial study of morality and moral development, Kohlberg concluded that humans move through six main stages divided into three levels, each one named for the way it relates to conventional views on moral dilemmas.

Pre-Conventional Level

> *"I'm sorry, but I don't want to end up*
> *in this super-jail like Wiccan."*
> —Cassie Lang, a.k.a. Stature[6]

A person using pre-conventional moral reasoning responds to cultural rules and understands the labels "good" and "bad," but actions and decisions are primarily a result of the person's own hedonistic consequences or the influence of those in power over the person.

- *Stage 1: Punishment and obedience orientation.* The physical consequences of the action determine whether it is good or bad. There is no concern with human value.
- *Stage 2: Naive instrumental hedonism.* What is right directly benefits and satisfies the decision-maker. Things are viewed in a pragmatic way.

The pre-conventional stages reflect decisions that are based on pleasure and pain. Two examples of decisions in *Civil War* that are based on Kohlberg's first stage occur when two minor characters make the jump from Captain America's team to

Iron Man's. When the hero Nighthawk pleads with Captain America to join Iron Man's side,[7] he argues that their allies' arrest and one hero's death should be enough to prove they are in the wrong. The heroine called Stature (Ant-Man's daughter Cassie Lang) says she does not want to go to jail like her friends,[8] and therefore the basis of her decision to join Iron Man and support registration is the fear of punishment.[9] Neither Nighthawk nor Stature mentions any indication of more advanced moral reasoning, such as respect for the underlying moral order. Their primary concern is personal safety.

As Iron Man works to gather supporters for the Superhuman Registration Act, he employs several tactics. One tactic is the emphasis on punishment and reward. For example, when he visits Luke Cage and Jessica Jones, he reminds them that the act can give them financial benefits and keep them out of jail.[10] Cage and Jones refuse to side with Iron Man, citing the types of role models they want to be for their daughter and their community.[11] Their decision to abstain from voting reflects the higher moral development found in stage 6, one that is centered on the dignity of others and universal rights.

Iron Man also appeals to stage 2 moral decision-making when he asks Emma Frost to help him get the X-Men's support. If the X-Men will join his side, he argues, they can win favor with the government. He understands the strained relationship mutants have had with authority, and he hopes Emma will take advantage of his proposition to further the needs and desires of the X-Men.[12] Unfortunately for him, his invitation falls on deaf ears as Emma claims neutrality; this is an example of avoiding the process of decision-making found in Kohlberg's second stage of moral development.

Conventional Level

"The public doesn't want masks and secret identities. They want to be safe when we're around, and there's no other way to win back their respect."
—Iron Man[13]

In conventional moral reasoning, people value the maintenance of social order, as in the family and community. There is a degree of conformity and loyalty to the existing social order.

- *Stage 3: Good-boy morality, maintaining good relations and approval of others.* Approval for being "nice" is a driving force. Conformity to social stereotypes emerges here.
- *Stage 4: Authority maintaining morality.* The emphasis is on following the law and performing one's duty as a member of the society to which the person belongs.

The majority of the moral decisions made in *Civil War* are classified in the conventional and post-conventional levels.[14] In the third stage, characters' actions are driven by societal acceptance and perception of being good. By advocating for the Superhuman Registration Act, Iron Man wins public favor.[15] People cheer his efforts, and the reinforcement from society suggests that he may be right in his choice. His alliance with a non–superhuman public figurehead helps guide him toward acting in a way that the public wants to see. Public opinion is not the only thing driving Iron Man: His decision to push the Superhuman Registration Act earns him high regard from several government officials, such as the president of the United States.[16]

Other heroes exhibit moral decisions characteristic of this stage. Spider–Man initially sides with Iron Man, and his actions are understood to be guided by good intentions.[17] She-Hulk, who is a lawyer and firm supporter of Iron Man, recognizes the act as a response to public opinion. Decisions made in this stage rely on the perception and approval of society in general.

Stage 4 of Kohlberg's moral development reflects a person's respect for the law and the authority figures behind it. It is not so much a fear of punishment for breaking the law as an understanding that maintaining the law maintains society. Iron Man brings up the importance of becoming "legitimate" in the eyes of society in general.[18] He sees this duty as an extension of his role as a protector. (There is also probably a hefty amount of guilt relating to the deaths of many children that initiated the enactment of the act.) By the end of *Civil War*, Iron Man becomes the authority figure others must respect and follow.[19] Iron Man is not fully confident in his deference to authority and law during this conflict. In conversations with his close confidants, there is an emphasis on just how difficult it is for him to support the Superhuman Registration Act.[20]

Captain America most notably does not operate in this stage. Aligning with stage 4 indicates that the person values the maintenance of social order above all else. When Captain America is called on by S.H.I.E.L.D. Director Maria Hill to uphold the social order, he refuses to act against his friends.[21] Heroes like Luke Cage and Daredevil are street-level protectors, he argues, and the law has the potential to harm them and their families. Hill does not see Captain America's refusal as a moral act; instead, she equates his behavior with that of a villain. Hill is not the only one who condemns Captain America's actions in breaking the law.[22]

Post-Conventional Level

*"Don't play politics with me, Hill. Super-heroes need to
stay above that stuff or Washington starts telling us who the
super-villains are."*
—Captain America[23]

Moral values and principles extend beyond the authority of
a group and exist separately from personal identification and
chosen societal groups.

- *Stage 5: Morality of contract and of democratically accepted
  law:* The right and moral action is dependent on
  personal values and opinions. Law is flexible in favor of
  social utility.
- *Stage 6: Morality of individual principles of conscience*:
  Morality is abstract rather than explicitly defined, and
  it operates on a universal level. There is an emphasis on
  human value and dignity.[24]

The fifth stage of moral development marks the crossover into
the post-conventional level, when people wrestle with moral
decisions from an individual and universal perspective. Despite
being on the run from the authorities, Captain America fulfills
his duty as a protector of others.[25] He and other heroes under-
ground continue to stop villains at the risk of being captured
by Hill and her S.H.I.E.L.D. agents. Captain America also
recognizes the flexibility of the law. When two minor villains
opt to join him in the fight against registration, the Punisher
immediately guns them down.[26] Captain America's reaction to
the Punisher's murders highlights the fact that he values their
lives more than he values strict rules.

Interestingly, Iron Man reveals that the Superhuman
Registration Act is more than an effort to save face.[27] The purpose

of the law is to allow for the continued protection and work of the superheroes. It acts as a compromise, an agreed-on set of standards to protect both humans and superhumans. Democratic law theoretically falls under stage 5 because of the critical examination of the laws and the way they benefit people overall.

The highest stage of moral development is often synonymous with civil disobedience. Ethical principles are universal and internalized. This is an area where Captain America thrives. His moral decisions in *Civil War* are primarily at stage 6. Captain America's primary stand is uncompromising freedom for all members of the superhero community.[28] His refusal to follow Maria Hill stems from his belief that it is wrong to arrest people who have done no harm.[29] Hill calls for obedience, and Captain America opts to follow his own guiding morality.

Spider-Man's initial choice to side with Iron Man and reveal his identity may be based on good intentions, but Captain America believes his actions may have endangered Spider-Man's wife and aunt.[30] He believes that Spider-Man has sacrificed the safety of his family for a law that does not respect the rights and privacy of superheroes.

Captain America's most significant moral decision comes at the end of the *Civil War* main series. During an all-out battle between the supporters of the act and those who oppose it, Captain America is restrained by a number of civilians. He uses this opportunity to stop and reflect on why he is fighting.[31] His main purpose in joining the conflict is to retain the freedom to act as a hero. The conflict has taken him far from that goal, and he changes his stance in favor of ending the costly, devastating battle and getting heroes back on the streets to maintain the peace and safety of others. Captain America, however, does criticize Iron Man for his actions, claiming that he never had to fight for freedom.[32] Iron Man's greatest sin, according to Captain America, is his willingness to compromise rather than demand freedom.[33]

Morality in the Real World

Kohlberg's development of these moral stages was heavily influenced by Piaget's stages of cognitive development and other theories. In his development of the theory, he determined that people move through the stages sequentially and do not regress.[34] An individual, though, can stop moral development at any stage. In fact, very few people ever make it to stage 5 or 6. Stage progression is tied to age or, more accurately, the development of a person. At the pre-conventional level, people are highly influenced by limited cognitive development and powerlessness. Younger people tend to be in the pre-conventional level, and older adults are more likely to function at a conventional or post-conventional level.

Consider your reaction to the moral dilemma featuring the husband and the druggist. The answer can be either yes or no, but the approach to the answer can reflect one of the six stages. For example:

- Stage 1: No, because he could get in trouble and be punished.
- Stage 2: Yes, because the wife wants to live and she might help him later.
- Stage 3: Yes, because the druggist is being unfair and the husband is a good husband who loves his wife.
- Stage 4: No, because the druggist owns the drugs and it is illegal to steal.
- Stage 5: No, because the druggist has the right to set the price. The husband has just cause to steal, but he is wrong legally.
- Stage 6: Yes, because the value of human life is greater than greed or material possessions.

COGNITIVE STAGES

Kohlberg's theory of moral development was influenced by Jean Piaget's looking at cognitive[35] and moral[36] development in children. Piaget's stages reflect both children's biological maturation and their social experiences.

- Sensorimotor (birth through 2 years): The child learns about the world through sensations. These children become aware that they are separate from their environment.
- Preoperational (2 years through 7 years): The child learns the meaning of language and how to communicate with others.
- Concrete operational (7 years through 11 years): The child learns reasoning skills and abstract thinking, including the ability to take perspectives.
- Formal operational (11 years and older): These children are able to think abstractly and utilize hypotheses to learn about their world.

Piaget's work laid the foundation for understanding that moral thinking is not static throughout development.[37]

These are examples of the reasoning that falls in line with each stage. Morality is far from being exact; it relies on people's cognitive development, their life experiences, and their interpretation of a moral dilemma. Morality research reveals that when the interests of personal needs and community collide, moral behavior is tied to the relationship a person has with his or her community.[38] This relationship can be the foundation for altruistic behaviors such as standing up for those who are unable or fighting for a larger cause than oneself.

So Who Is Right?

The decisions made by Iron Man, Captain America, and those influenced by them provide a range of responses that highlight Kohlberg's stages of moral development. At times, their adamant focus on the conflict keeps them from remembering their values and principles, but the reasons and rationales behind their actions reveal what Captain America and Iron Man value most. In the end, both heroes want to protect their community, and their approaches demonstrate how difficult it can be to make moral decisions.

Comic Book References

Civil War #1–7 (2006–2007). Script: M. Millar. Art: S. McNiven, D. Vines, M. Hollowell, & C. Eliopoulos.

Civil War: The Confession #1 (2007). Script: B. M. Bendis. Art: A. Maleev, J. Villarrubia, & C. Eliopoulos.

Hawkeye #1 (2012). "Lucky: A Clint Barton/Hawkeye Adventure." Script: M. Fraction. Art: D. Aja.

Iron Man #13 (2006). Script: D. Knauf. Art: P. Zircher, S. Hanna, E. Delgado, & J. Caramagna.

New Avengers #21 (2006). Script: B. M. Bendis. Art: H. Chaykin, J. Pimentel, D. Stewart, & Comicraft.

New Avengers #22 (2006). Script: B. M. Bendis. Art: L. F. Yu, D. McCraig, & Comicraft.

References

Dunlop, W. L., Walker, L. J., & Matsuba, M. K. (2013). The development of moral motivation across the adult lifespan. *European Journal of Developmental Psychology,* *10*(2), 285–300.

Gould, M., & Howson, A. (2011). Piaget's stages of cognitive development. In Salem Press (Eds.), *Sociology reference guide: The process of socialization* (pp. 29–38). Pasadena, CA: Salem Press.

Kohlberg, L. (1958). *The development of modes of thinking and choices in years 10–16.* PhD dissertation. Chicago, IL: University of Chicago.

Kohlberg, L. (1963). The development of children's orientation toward a moral order: I. Sequence in the development of moral thought. *Vita Humana, 6*(1–2), 11–33.

Kohlberg, L. (1973). The claim to moral adequacy of a highest stage of moral judgment. *Journal of Philosophy, 70*(18), 630–646.

Piaget, J. (1930). *The child's conception of physical reality.* New York, NY: Routledge.

Piaget, J. (1932). *The moral development of the child.* New York, NY: Harcourt Brace Jovanovich.

Piaget, J. (1954). *The construction of reality in the child.* New York, NY: Basic.

Walker, L. J. (1982). The sequentiality of Kohlberg's stages of moral development. *Child Development, 53*(5), 1330–1336.

Notes

1. Kohlberg (1963).
2. *Hawkeye* #1 (2012).
3. *Civil War* #6 (2006).
4. Kohlberg (1958).
5. Kohlberg (1963).
6. *Civil War* #4 (2006).
7. *Civil War* #4 (2006).
8. *Civil War* #4 (2006).
9. *Civil War* #3 & #5 (2006).
10. *New Avengers* #22 (2006).
11. *New Avengers* #22 (2006).
12. *Civil War* #3 (2006).
13. *Civil War* #3 (2006).
14. Kohlberg (1973).
15. *Civil War* #2 (2006).
16. *Iron Man* #13 (2006).
17. *Civil War* #5 (2006).
18. *Civil War* #1 (2006).
19. *Civil War* #7 (2007).
20. *Iron Man* #13 (2006).
21. *Civil War* #1 (2006).
22. *Civil War* #3 (2006).
23. *Civil War* #1 (2006).
24. Kohlberg (1963).
25. *Civil War* #2 (2006).
26. *Civil War* #6 (2006).
27. *Civil War* #6 (2006).

28. *New Avengers* #21 (2006).
29. *Civil War* #1 (2006).
30. *Civil War* #3 (2006).
31. *Civil War* #7 (2006).
32. *Civil War: The Confession* #1 (2007).
33. *Civil War: The Confession* #1 (2007).
34. Walker (1982).
35. Piaget (1930, 1954).
36. Piaget (1932).
37. Gould & Howson (2011).
38. Dunlop et al. (2013).

Trauma can change people. It tears some down but pushes others to grow and find purpose. Posttraumatic stress disorder is one well-known consequence that many people experience, but there is also a phenomenon known as posttraumatic growth. The way a person copes with suffering may be what defines a hero.

CHAPTER TWO

TRAUMA SHAPES A SUPERHERO

JANINA SCARLET
AND JENNA BUSCH

"We create our own demons."
—Tony Stark[1]

"A traumatic event doesn't doom us to suffer indefinitely.
Instead, we can use it as a springboard to unleash our best
qualities and lead happier lives."
—game researcher/psychologist Jane McGonigal[2]

Most people struggle with painful loss or trauma at some point in their lives. Well-developed fictional characters may mirror this fact, and it has become increasingly common for writers to integrate tragedy into superheroes' backgrounds.[3] Having tragically lost loved ones at early ages and having experienced violent traumas, both Steve Rogers and Tony Stark are nevertheless able to become superheroes and follow their own core values of helping others. People who experience tragic loss and later experience severe trauma are at risk of developing a physical or mental health disorder such as *posttraumatic stress disorder* (PTSD),[4] although some follow a pattern of *posttraumatic growth* in which trauma causes them to find purpose and grow as individuals.[5] What factors help people recover from tragedies and become heroic? What path do heroic individuals take to help themselves recover and become the very best versions of themselves?

Posttraumatic Stress Disorder

About half of all people are exposed to traumatic events at some point in their lives, but not everyone who goes through a trauma develops PTSD.[6] Approximately 10% of women and 4% of men develop this disorder.[7] Both Steve and Tony lose their parents, both almost die in several combat situations, both see friends die,[8] and both fight aliens and other enemies capable of conquering or destroying the world.[9] Although both are affected by these events, only Tony seems to develop PTSD.[10]

Experiential Avoidance

Among the PTSD symptoms listed in the sidebar, avoidance of any difficult experiences related to the trauma (sometimes referred to as *experiential avoidance*) is one of the biggest contributors to the development of PTSD.[11] Experiential avoidance can manifest in many different ways. For example, someone undergoing trauma may stop socializing with his or her friends, in particular those who might have been involved in the traumatic event.[12] Other people attempt to numb their emotions by abusing alcohol or other substances.[13] Tony first struggles with alcoholism after his suit, which has been reprogrammed by an

PTSD SYMPTOMS: WHY CAN'T TONY SLEEP?

PTSD is diagnosed when a person experiences a traumatic, potentially life-threatening event and subsequently shows certain kinds of symptoms that interfere with life functioning. This can be a direct experience or an indirect one, such as when an individual learns of a loved one's trauma. To be diagnosed, the person must experience the following symptoms for at least a month:[14]

- *Intrusions:* Reexperiencing the traumatic event through flashbacks or nightmares. For example, Tony Stark struggles with both when he remembers fighting alien invaders in New York.[15]
- *Avoidance:* Avoiding any potential reminders of the traumatic situation, including people, places, and thoughts. Tony stays up for 72 hours straight to work on a new suit to avoid having anxiety attacks and nightmares.[16] In many stories, he uses alcohol to escape his problems.[17] Similarly, Steve uses avoidance when he refuses to date or be reminded of his lost love, Agent Peggy Carter, after his trauma of being frozen in ice.[18]
- *Negative changes in the person's mood or thoughts:* Tony Stark seems to demonstrate this when he is seemingly depressed and unmotivated and struggles with panic attacks. In the film *Iron Man 3*, Tony struggles with severe panic attacks.[19] Overwhelmed by a number of his combat experiences in the comic book, Tony lashes out at his butler, the human version of Jarvis, until Jarvis quits.[20]
- *Increased arousal symptoms:* Hypervigilance, difficulty sleeping, and irritability. Tony struggles with all these symptoms after the Battle of New York and even puts on his Iron Man suit in his sleep.[21] In the comics, Tony's distrust of his fiancée is apparent when he plants *nanites* (programmable microscopic robotic devices) in her body.[22]

evil scientist, kills a foreign ambassador.[23] Overwhelmed by guilt, Tony drinks to escape his pain.[24] Similarly, Steve Rogers uses excessive exercise in an attempt to cope with his new life shortly after he recovers from being frozen instead of heading out immediately to investigate the new world in which he finds himself.[25] Most people who engage in experiential avoidance may experience short-term relief from their symptoms. However, in the long term these avoidance behaviors might not only prolong PTSD but could also lead to the development of other mental health and physical disorders.[26]

Negative Effects of Trauma

In addition to developing PTSD, tragic losses and painful events can lead to other mental health issues, such as depression, substance abuse, and anxiety.[27] Having lost his parents at an early age, nearly getting killed himself, and feeling guilty about the lives he could not save lead Tony to develop a substance abuse disorder and lash out at the people closest to him.[28]

Prolonged effects of trauma can affect a person's physiology. For example, traumatic events may result in cell death (*apoptosis*) in the memory-processing region of the brain (the *hippocampus*) [29] as well as stomach issues and difficulty with breathing and concentrating.[30] After the Battle of New York, Tony seems to be experiencing some of these physiological sensations, specifically, difficulty breathing during a panic attack he has as some children come up to ask for his autograph. He inadvertently writes, "Erin help me," on one of the drawings and breaks the crayon he has been using. Tony's trauma symptoms seem to be affecting his physiology and impairing his ability to concentrate.[31]

In addition, exposure to traumatic events and long-term stressors can shorten a person's life. Researchers have found that people who have been exposed to trauma have shorter telomeres. *Telomeres* are the tail ends of chromosomes left over after DNA replication. The shorter these are, the shorter a person's life seems to be.[32] People who have experienced a lot of trauma, as Steve and Tony have, are more likely to develop shorter telomeres, potentially shortening their life spans.

The Superhero Resilience

Although exposure to trauma and stress can decrease a person's life span,[33] this effect seems to occur mainly in people who stress about being stressed. When people are able to form meaningful social connections with others even in the face of stress or trauma, they are less likely to die prematurely and more likely to feel physically and emotionally better. This is due largely to a hormone, *oxytocin,* stored in the pituitary gland. This hormone is released when people are bonding with others. It also has protective effects on an individual's physical and emotional health.[34] The protective effects of social support are especially apparent when Tony is in the midst of his depression and seeks out the support of his then-girlfriend, Bethany Cabe. Bethany confides in him about her former husband's struggle with addiction and provides the encouragement that helps Tony begin his recovery.[35] Steve Rogers also frequently seeks the support of his friend and fellow soldier Bucky Barnes[36] as well as his friend Sam Wilson (the Falcon),[37] both of whom offer him the support he needs to feel less alone.

Perhaps one of the key factors in developing resilience is to live life in accordance with one's own core values and with minimum regrets. There are five regrets people most commonly report toward the end of their lives:

- Working too much.
- Not doing enough activities that make them happy.

• Not being true to themselves.
• Not following their true dreams and core values.
• Not connecting/keeping in touch with friends enough.[38]

Tony Stark and especially Steve Rogers are able to follow their core values in protecting others as well as being true to themselves and their friends. Although they work a lot, they also participate in activities that make them happy. For instance, Tony, Steve, and the other Avengers socialize and even joke about who is worthy to pick up Thor's hammer.[39] (In the comics, Captain America has lifted it and therefore is worthy.[40])

Overall, when people are altruistic and are able to connect with others they love and activities they enjoy, they appear to be more likely to live long and healthy lives.[41] For instance, during a date night with Pepper, Tony appears much calmer and happier than usual.[42] After defeating Ultron, Steve confides in Tony that he used to want a family and a normal life but that he has come to accept the Avengers' headquarters as his home and his friends as his family.[43] By connecting with people they love as well as having a sense of purpose, these courageous men are able to become superheroes.

Being a Superhero Is Healthy

Both Tony and Steve are shaped by trauma early, losing their parents at a young age and nearly losing their lives in war. Though they have different reasons for doing so, both find ways to become heroes, and this helps both of them cope with their losses. Research on altruism suggests that people who are altruistic, as superheroes often are, tend to lead healthier and happier lives.[44] By forming meaningful social connections and following their core values, both Tony and Steve are able to manage their losses and trauma symptoms more effectively. For Tony, this act of altruism entails building machines to save the world. For Steve, his sense of duty and love of his country encourages him to volunteer for the Super-Soldier project, which subsequently makes him Captain America. Although they repeatedly face trauma throughout their careers, they are able to build resilience and overcome even the most painful experiences.

Comic Book References

The Avengers #4 (1964, March). "Captain America Joins the Avengers!" Script: S. Lee. Art: J. Kirby & G. Roussos.

Captain America Comics #1 (1941). "Meet Captain America." Script: J. Simon. Art: J. Kirby & A. Liederman.

Iron Man #124 (1979). "Pieces of Hate." Script: D. Michelinie. Art: J. Romita Jr., B. Layton, B. McLeod, & B. Wiacek.

Iron Man #125 (1979). "The Monaco Prelude." Script: D. Michelinie. Art: J. Romita Jr. & B. Layton.

Iron Man #126 (1979). "The Hammer Strikes!" Script: D. Michelinie. Art: J. Romita Jr. & B. Layton.

Iron Man #127 (1979). "A Man's Home Is His Battlefield . . ." Script: D. Michelinie. Art: J. Romita Jr. & B. Layton.

Iron Man #128 (1979). "Demon in a Bottle." Script: D. Michelinie & B. Layton. Art: J. Romita Jr. & B. Layton.

Tales of Suspense #39 (1963). "Iron Man Is Born!" Script: S. Lee. Art: J. Kirby, & D. Heck.

Thor #390 (1988). "The Hero and the Hammer!" Script: T. DeFalco. Art: R. Frenz & B. Breeding.

The Ultimates 2 #10. (2006). "Axis of Evil." Script: M. Millar. Art: B. Hitch. L. Martin, & P. Neary.

Other References

Abdelnoor, A., & Hollins, S. (2004). The effect of childhood bereavement on secondary school performance. *Educational Psychology in Practice, 20*(1), 43–54.

American Psychiatric Association (2013). *Diagnostic and statistical manual of mental disorders* (DSM-5) (5th ed.). Washington, DC: American Psychiatric Association.

Andelic, N., Sigurdardottir, S., Schanke, A. K., Sandvik, L., Sveen, U., & Roe, C. (2010). Disability, physical health and mental health 1 year after traumatic brain injury. *Disability and Rehabilitation, 32*(13), 1122–1131.

Black, K., & Lobo, M. (2008). A conceptual review of family resilience factors. *Journal of Family Nursing, 14*(1), 33–55.

Bossini, L., Tavanti, M., Lombardelli, A., Calossi, S., Polizzotto, N. R., Galli, R., Pieraccini, F., & Castrogiovanni, P. (2007). Changes in hippocampal volume in patients with post-traumatic stress disorder after sertraline treatment. *Journal of Clinical Psychopharmacology, 27*(2), 233–235.

Del Gaizo, A. L., Elhai, J. D., & Weaver, T. L. (2011). Posttraumatic stress disorder, poor physical health and substance use behaviors in a national trauma-exposed sample. *Psychiatry Research, 188*(3), 390–395.

Diehl, M., & Hay, E. L. (2010). Risk and resilience factors in coping with daily stress in adulthood: The role of age, self-concept incoherence, and personal control. *Developmental Psychology, 46*(5), 1132–1146.

Dowdney, L. (2000). Annotation: Childhood bereavement following parental death. *Journal of Child Psychology and Psychiatry, 41*(7), 819–830.

Fingeroth, D. (2005). *Superman on the couch: What superheroes really tell us about ourselves and our society.* New York, NY: Continuum.

Frueh, B. C., Turner, S. M., Beidel, D. C., & Cahill, S. P. (2001). Assessment of social functioning in combat veterans with PTSD. *Aggression and Violent Behavior, 6*(1), 79–90.

Glaser, D. (2000). Child abuse and neglect and the brain—a review. *Journal of Child Psychology and Psychiatry, 41*(1), 97–116.

Hijazi, A. M., Keith, J. A., & O'Brien, C. (2015). Predictors of posttraumatic growth in a multiwar sample of U. S. combat veterans. *Journal of Peace Psychology, 21*(3), 395–408.

Hofmann, S. G., Litz, B. T., & Weathers, F. W. (2003). Social anxiety, depression, and PTSD in Vietnam veterans. *Journal of Anxiety Disorders, 17*(5), 573–582.

Jacobs, S. (1996). Complicated grief as a disorder distinct from bereavement-related depression and anxiety: A replication study. *American Journal of Psychiatry, 153*(11), 1484–1486.

Jacobson, I. G., Ryan, M. K., Hooper, T. J., Smith, T. C., Amoroso, P. J., Boyko, E. J., Gackstetter, D. G., Wells, T. S., & Bell, N. S. (2008). Alcohol use and alcohol-related problems before and after military combat deployment. *JAMA: Journal of the American Medical Association, 300*(6), 663–675.

Johnson, H., & Thompson, A. (2008). The development and maintenance of post-traumatic stress disorder (PTSD) in civilian adult survivors of war trauma and torture: A review. *Clinical Psychology Review, 28*(1), 36–47.

Kikuchi, A., Shimizu, K., Nibuya, M., Hiramoto, T., Kanda, Y., Tanaka, T., Watanabe, Y., Takahashi, Y., & Nomura, S. (2008). Relationship between post-traumatic stress disorder-like behavior and reduction of hippocampal 5-bromo-2-deoxyuridine-positive cells after inescapable shock in rats. *Psychiatry and Clinical Neurosciences, 62*(6), 713–720.

Langley, T. (2013, May 4). *Does Iron Man 3's hero suffer posttraumatic stress disorder? Psychology Today:* https://www.psychologytoday.com/blog/beyond-heroes-and -villains/201305/does-iron-man-3s-hero-suffer-posttraumatic-stress-disorder.

Lehman, D. R., Ellard, J. H., & Wortman, C. B. (1986). Social support for the bereaved: Recipients' and providers' perspectives on what is helpful. *Journal of Consulting and Clinical Psychology, 54*(4), 438.

Letamendi, A. (2013, May 10). *Iron Man: A terrible privilege.* Under the Mask Online: http://www.underthemaskonline.com/iron-man-a-terrible-privilege/.

Lohr, J. B., Palmer, B. W., Eidt, C. A., Aailaboyina, S., Mausbach, B. T., Wolkowitz, O. M., Thorpe, S. R., & Jeste, D. V. (2015). Is post-traumatic stress disorder associated with premature senescence? A review of the literature. *American Journal of Geriatric Psychiatry, 23*(7), 709–725.

McAllister, T. W., Flashman, L. A., McDonald, B. C., & Saykin, A. J. (2006). Mechanisms of working memory dysfunction after mild and moderate TBI: Evidence from functional MRI and neurogenetics. *Journal of Neurotrauma, 23*(10), 1450–1467.

McCormack, L., & McKellar, L. (2015). Adaptive growth following terrorism: Vigilance and anger as facilitators of posttraumatic growth in the aftermath of the Bali bombings. *Traumatology, 21*(2), 71–81.

McGonigal, J. (2012). *The game that can give you 10 extra years of life* [video file]. TED: https://www.ted.com/talks/jane_mcgonigal_the_game_that_can_give_you_10_extra_years_of_life?language=en.

McGonigal, J. (2015). *Superbetter: A revolutionary approach to getting stronger, happier, braver, and more resilient.* New York, NY: Penguin Press.

McGonigal, K. (2015). *The upside of stress: Why stress is good for you, and how to get good at it.* New York, NY: Penguin.

National Center for PTSD (2014, November 10). How common is PTSD? U.S. Department of Veteran Affairs: http://www.ptsd.va.gov/public/PTSD-overview/basics/how-common-is-ptsd.asp.

Pacella, M. L., Hruska, B., & Delahanty, D. L. (2013). The physical health consequences of PTSD and PTSD symptoms: A meta-analytic review. *Journal of Anxiety Disorders, 27*(1), 33–46.

Park, C. L., & Ai, A. L. (2006). Meaning making and growth: New directions for research on survivors of trauma. *Journal of Loss and Trauma, 11*(5), 389–407.

Plumb, J. C., Orsillo, S. M., & Luterek, J. A. (2004). A preliminary test of the role of experiential avoidance in post-event functioning. *Journal of Behavior Therapy and Experimental Psychiatry, 35*(3), 245–257.

Post, S. G. (2005). Altruism, happiness, and health: It's good to be good. *International Journal of Behavioral Medicine, 12*(2), 66–77.

Poulin, M. J., Brown, S. L., Dillard, A. J., & Smith, D. M. (2013). Giving to others and the association between stress and mortality. *American Journal of Public Health, 103*(9), 1649–1655.

Poulin, M. J., & Holman, E. A. (2013). Helping hands, healthy body? Oxytocin receptor gene and prosocial behavior interact to buffer the association between stress and physical health. *Hormones and Behavior, 63*(3), 510–517.

Prigerson, H. G., Shear, M. K., Jacobs, S. C., Reynolds, C., Maciejewski, P. K., Davidson, J. R., Rosenheck, R., Pikonis, P. A., Wortman, C. B., Williams, J. B., Widiger, T. A., Kupfer, F. E., & Zisook, S. (1999). Consensus criteria for traumatic grief. A preliminary empirical test. *British Journal of Psychiatry, 174*(1), 67–73.

Puterman, E., Lin, J., Krauss, J., Blackburn, E. H., & Epel, E. S. (2015). Determinants of telomere attrition over 1 year in healthy older women: Stress and health behaviors matter. *Molecular Psychiatry, 20*(4), 529–535.

Romagnoli, A. S., & Pagnucci, G. S. (2013). *Enter the superheroes: American values, culture, and the canon of superhero literature.* Lanham, MD: Scarecrow.

Scarbro, N. (2013, January 30). *America's superheroes: Traumatic experiences lead to heroism?* The Graphic Novel: http://graphicnovel.umwblogs.org/2013/01/30/americas-superheroes-traumatic-experiences-lead-to-heroism/.

Schwartz, C., Meisenhelder, J. B., Ma, Y., & Reed, G. (2003). Altruistic social interest behaviors are associated with better mental health. *Psychosomatic Medicine, 65*(5), 778–785.

Shakespeare-Finch, J., & Lurie-Beck, J. (2014). A meta-analytic clarification of the relationship between posttraumatic growth and symptoms of posttraumatic stress disorder. *Journal of Anxiety Disorders, 28*(2), 223–229.

Van Slyke, J. (n.d.). *Post-traumatic growth (white paper).* Naval Center Combat and Operational Stress Control: http://www.med.navy.mil/sites/nmcsd/nccosc/item%28changed%29/post-traumatic-growth-white-paper/index.aspx.

Ware, B. (2012). *The top five regrets of the dying: A life transformed by the dearly departing.* Carlsbad, CA: Hay House.

Wheeler, I. (2001). Parental bereavement: The crisis of meaning. *Death Studies, 25*(1), 51–66.

Notes

1. *Iron Man 3* (2013 motion picture).
2. J. McGonigal (2012).
3. Fingeroth (2005); Romagnolli & Pagnucci (2013); Scarbro (2013).
4. Prigerson et al. (1999).
5. Hijazi et al. (2015); McCormack & McKellar (2015); Shakespeare-Finch & Lurie-Beck (2014).
6. National Center for PTSD (2014).
7. National Center for PTSD (2014).
8. e.g., *Avengers #4* (1964); *Tales of Suspense* #39 (1963).
9. *The Avengers* (2012 motion picture).
10. e.g., *Iron Man 3* (2013 motion picture); Langley (2013); Letamendi (2013).
11. Plumb et al. (2004).
12. Frueh et al. (2001); Hoffmann et al. (2003).
13. Del Gaizo et al (2011); Jacobson et al. (2008).
14. American Psychiatric Association (2013).
15. *Iron Man 3* (2013 motion picture).
16. *Iron Man 3* (2013 motion picture).
17. *Iron Man* #125–128 (1979).
18. *Captain America: The Winter Soldier* (2014 motion picture).
19. *Iron Man 3* (2013 motion picture).
20. *Iron Man* #127 (1979).
21. *Iron Man 3* (2013 motion picture).
22. *The Ultimates 2* #10 (2006).
23. *Iron Man* #124 (1979).
24. *Iron Man* #125–128 (1979).
25 *The Avengers* (2012 motion picture).
26. Plumb et al. (2004).
27. Jacobs (1996).
28. *Iron Man* #127 (1979); *Iron Man 3* (2013 motion picture).
29. Bossini et al. (2007); Kikuchi et al. (2008).
30. Del Gaizo et al. (2011); Pacella et al. (2013).
31. *Iron Man 3* (2013 motion picture).
32. Lohr et al. (2015); Puterman et al. (2015).
33. Poulin et al. (2013).
34. K. McGonigal (2015); Poulin & Holman (2013).
35. *Iron Man* #128 (1979).
36. *Captain America Comics* #1 (1941).

37. *Captain America: The Winter Soldier* (2014 motion picture).
38. Ware (2012).
39. *Avengers: Age of Ultron* (2015 motion picture).
40. *Thor* #390 (1988).
41. J. McGonigal (2015); K. McGonigal (2015); Post (2005).
42. *The Avengers* (2012 motion picture).
43. *Avengers: Age of Ultron* (2015 motion picture).
44. Post (2005).

Even a person who has grown a conscience and has the ability to overcome trauma needs to take certain steps to make any of that matter. Positive psychology does more than ask questions about how those who rise to the occasion during times of trouble differ from bystanders who do not. It offers a plan: a series of steps for turning good intentions into actions.

CHAPTER THREE

WHAT IT TAKES TO BE A SUPERHERO

PATRICK O'CONNOR

"I don't want to kill anyone. I don't like bullies, I don't care where they're from."
—Steve Rogers[1]

"True heroism is remarkably sober, very undramatic. It is not the urge to surpass all others at whatever cost, but the urge to serve others at whatever cost."
—tennis champion Arthur Ashe[2]

Positive psychology has illuminated ways in which anybody can become a hero. Being heroic is not a trait or status; rather, it is something people can strive for and achieve in a number of different ways. What makes Captain America and Iron Man such great heroes is the fact that they highlight two very different paths toward achieving heroism on a fantastic scale. Steve Rogers has a heart bigger than the scrawny frame that contains it. He does not want to kill enemies because of who they are; rather, he wants to oppose them because of what they do[3]—a moral stance that becomes the centerpiece for his development from Steve Rogers, ordinary person, into Captain America, extraordinary hero.[4] In contrast, Tony Stark's growth into Iron Man results from his almost losing everything before choosing to grow beyond that loss. Both characters illustrate the ability to become super; however, a person does not need Super-Soldier Serum or access to incredible machinery to become heroic.

Becoming Heroic

Some psychologists are dissatisfied that so much of psychological science has focused on what is wrong with people. They believe that if psychology can develop a rich understanding of illness and what it takes to develop it, psychology also can develop a rich understanding of wellness and what it takes to develop it. These psychologists focus on *positive psychology*, which explores how positive emotions and positive character develop.[5]

Just as other psychological research emphasizes mental illness and how to move away from it, positive psychologists focus on mental wellness and how to move toward it. Altruism is a major factor in feeling good about oneself, and possibly nothing is more altruistic than being heroic. Let's explore three steps Steve Rogers and Tony Stark take to become heroes and consider how those steps apply to others.

Step 1: Listen to Your Anxiety

Although the term *call to adventure* typically refers to American mythologist Joseph Campbell's first stage in the *monomyth* (the "one myth" represented in heroic stories through history, the Hero's Journey[6]), it also can be used to describe the sense a person feels when something wrong has been done and this person realizes that he or she can do something about it.[7] People tend to feel very uncomfortable when they learn of their own unethical behaviors, and this discomfort is a form of *cognitive dissonance*. The conflict between a person's sense of character (e.g., "I am a good person") and the actions that contradict sense (e.g., "I did something wrong") creates an anxiety that might be relieved if the person changes his or her sense of character or behavior. Recognizing one's desire to maintain a favorable sense of self, the only course of action is to behave in a way that is in line with this identity.

Steve Rogers encounters this anxiety offscreen (*off-panel* in comics) when he is deciding whether to make another attempt to enlist in the army during World War II.[8] We could suppose Steve often finds himself sitting at home, keenly aware of the sacrifices men and women are making overseas while he feels helpless to contribute. This anxiety can be a very strong motivator. The worse a person feels about a situation in which he or she is involved, the more responsible that person feels for the outcome.[9] In fact, Steve voices this very concern to his best friend, Bucky Barnes: "There are men laying down their lives. I got no right to do any less than them."[10] Even when the scope expands to a grander scale, simply learning about the ways in which people blindly obey authority—even when it goes against their character—leads people to feel responsible for resolving societal issues and developing a sense of civil courage. *Civil courage* is "an inclination to intervene and/or oppose a majority opinion in a situation on the basis of one's authentic values while taking into account disapproval by authorities and social rejection."[11] In other words, people with civil courage stand up for what they believe regardless of social pressure. Steve thinks of himself as a defender of those who need help, and he is not going to let rejection lead him to inaction. Listening to his own anxiety, Steve continues to attempt to enlist, to bring himself closer to helping the bullied.

Stanley Milgram's experiments on obedience demonstrated that the majority of people will behave out of character when instructed to by a person they perceive to be in a position of authority.[12] These were not mild changes in behavior: The participants thought they were seriously injuring another person! In this experiment, Milgram enlisted two actors who deceived the participants into thinking one was an experimenter with authority and the other was another participant. The experiment was rigged so that the real participant would always be assigned the role of "teacher" and the fake participant would always be assigned the role of "learner." The teacher taught word pairs to the learner and asked the learner to recall the pairs. Whenever the learner got it right, the teacher continued down the list of terms. Every time the learner got it wrong, the teacher administered a small electric shock to the learner. For every wrong answer, the teacher would increase the voltage of the electric shock. (The fake participants were not really shocked, but the real participants thought they were. No learners were harmed in the making of Milgram's study.)

When psychiatrists were asked how many people would go all the way to the end of the shock box voltage (which was labeled "450 Volts, XXX"), their answer was fewer than 1%.[13] When I ask my own students to raise their hands if they believe they would go all the way to the end of the box, I'm lucky to see even a couple hands raised. However, the experiment and its replications have yielded results in which over 50% of participants essentially "killed" their learners.[14]

Steve Rogers exemplifies this disobedience in many ways. From his rejection of Nick Fury and S.H.I.E.L.D.'s idea of surveillance and violent suppression of crime[15] to his conflict with Iron Man over the federal act requiring superheroes to register with the government,[16] Steve is not afraid to stand up for what he believes. He does that despite any pressure he might feel from both his allies and his superiors.

Social pressure can be incredibly powerful, but it is important to listen to that "something is wrong" feeling if you find your-self in a situation in which you are being asked to do something that goes against your values. This cognitive dissonance could be trying to tell you that there is a call to adventure, a call to take action against what is being asked of you in that moment.

Step 2: Connect with a Feeling of Transcendence

Turning one's attention outward, away from actions that lead to personal gain, can lead a person to become more altruistic—more giving of himself or herself—in many different ways. When we increase our sense of awe, a feeling tied to a sense of being part of something bigger, we become more prosocial, more ethical, and more generous.[17] By increasing this sense of connectedness, we also promote the growth of a sense of global scale within us. That is, feeling small in such a big world helps put our problems and concerns into perspective and thus leads to us seek more opportunities to help others.

Tony Stark experiences a profound feeling of transcen-dence when he is taken captive in his origin story.[18] Before his capture, Tony learns that the opponents of American troops in a foreign country use weapons manufactured by his own Stark Industries.[19] While Tony is held prisoner, his captors' leader orders him to develop new weapons for his army, but Tony decides instead to create a suit of armor to aid him in his escape.

By increasing a sense of awe, we can decrease our sense of entitlement. People who feel entitled believe that they must be given what they think they are owed at the expense of

The *Character Strengths and Virtues* (CSV) handbook "describes and classifies strengths and virtues that enable human thriving."[20] These virtues are personality traits that come from a place of high moral or ethical standards within each of us. The CSV contains the following six virtues:

Virtue	Definition
Wisdom and knowledge	Acquiring and using knowledge
Courage	Achieving goals despite resistance or barriers
Humanity	Caring for others
Justice	Developing a healthy life in the community by being fair and leading by example
Temperance	Being modest and doing things in moderation
Transcendence	Connecting with a meaning larger than oneself

Tony Stark shows wisdom, knowledge, and courage when he uses his expertise to create suits of armor and develop a new form of renewable energy. Steve Rogers shows humanity, justice, and temperance by leading the Avengers, defending the powerless, and giving credit to others when it is due. As heroes, both illustrate transcendence by using their strengths to act for the betterment of humankind. Superheroes like Captain America and Iron Man serve as excellent examples of key virtues all of us can adopt to make our lives more fulfilling.

the relationship with the person from whom they expect the reward. An example of this could be a person who pushes his chair in at a restaurant and then expects the server to thank him for that action. Instead of being satisfied with his gesture of helping the wait staff, he feels it necessary to receive recognition and may even make the server uncomfortable with a dirty look if he does not receive it. By detaching concerns normally associated with ourselves, we can behave more *sociocentrically* (for the betterment of society) as opposed to *egocentrically* (for the betterment of oneself).

After his escape, Tony probably discovers his own smallness of self. Instead of focusing on work for personal gain by turning a blind eye to the fact that his weapons are being sold to armies that oppose the United States, he learns of his contribution to both sides in the same war and decides to make a change. A person can find greater reward in behaving sociocentrically while staying rooted in ethical behavior. In an impassioned speech to the press, Tony states, "I saw young Americans killed by the very weapons I created to defend them, to protect them, and I saw that I had become part of a system that was comfortable with zero accountability. . . . I have more to offer this world than just making things that blow up."[21] He announces that he is shutting down the weapons-manufacturing division of Stark Industries to focus instead on the development of the arc reactor to bring sustainable energy to the world. Heroes help because they can see their own ability to help others without the need for praise, recognition, or reward.

Step 3: Fight the Bystander Effect

When people are around others and an opportunity to help a stranger presents itself, the *bystander effect* is an unfortunate likelihood that prevents onlookers from taking action.[22] This is a consequence of inaction that can result from a fear of doing the wrong thing or making a fool of oneself in a challenging situation. People who fight the bystander effect have an opportunity to be heroic by taking action for the betterment of someone in need regardless of the potential sacrifice by the helper.

The bystander effect gained attention following the murder of Kitty Genovese in 1964. While the killer spent over 30 minutes stabbing her on a residential street in New York City, 38 witnesses supposedly looked on and did nothing to help her, not even making a telephone call to the police.[23] Whether there really were so many passive observers is a subject of dispute,[24] but there is no disputing the fact that none called for help. Some of the witnesses might have struggled with a concern for safety (e.g. "Frankly, we were afraid"), apathy (e.g. "I was tired, I went back to bed"), or denial (e.g. "We thought it was a lover's quarrel"). This effect has been demonstrated in several studies over a wide variety of conditions.

Bystanders are a common sight in superhero stories. Before becoming Captain America, Steve Rogers chases after a gun-toting sabateur while others back away in fear.[25] Even when the man takes a boy hostage, Steve is the only person moving toward the dangerous situation to save the boy. When the Avengers fight throughout New York City, the public is seen in the background watching helplessly.[26] However, the moment is brief. Steve Rogers is pinned inside a bus by machine-gun fire, and witnesses start helping the injured out of the bus to safety.[27] We may not have Super-Soldier Serum, high-tech suits of armor, or a vibranium shield, but we can use the skills and opportunities afforded to us to help those in need. Anyone can help a person to safety, but what matters more is whether that anyone is you.

Where to Go From Here

Being heroic is not about using superpowers or tapping into limitless wealth with a symbol on your chest. It's about taking three key steps to make the world a better place.

Listening to your anxiety can help illuminate where your attention needs to be drawn. If you feel tense about a situation in which you are involved, take the time to explore why you feel uncomfortable and how your actions could remedy the situation even if they go against the majority opinion. If something feels morally wrong, take the opportunity to address it.

Connecting with a feeling of transcendence entails putting your problems in a larger perspective. When people focus on sociocentric (society) concerns as opposed to egocentric (self) concerns, they tend to behave more ethically and report greater satisfaction when attempting to solve a problem. Even though our attention tends to focus on what is wrong within ourselves, we find a great deal of satisfaction when we turn that attention to others and their issues.

Fighting the bystander effect means taking action regardless of who else is around you. When someone is in danger, we must set aside our fears of embarrassment and determine what we can do to help. It can be as simple as helping a person up, calling 911, or asking if someone would like assistance in a position of need. Steve does this regardless of the serum flowing through his veins, and Tony does it regardless of the suit he is wearing.

The next time you find yourself in a situation in which you can help, think, "What would a hero like Captain America or Iron Man do?"

Comic Book References

Captain America Comics #1 (1941). "Meet Captain America." Script: J. Simon. Art: J. Kirby & A. Liederman.

Civil War #1 (2006). Script: M. Millar. Art: S. Nivens & D. Vines.

Iron Man #275 (1991). "The Dragon Seed Saga, Part IV: Dragon Doom." Script: J. Byrne. Art: P. Ryan & B. Wiacek.

Tales of Suspense #39 (1963). "Iron Man is Born!" Script: S. Lee. Art: J. Kirby & D. Heck.

Other References

Campbell, J. (1949). *The hero with a thousand faces.* New York, NY: Pantheon.

Darley, J. M., & Latané, B. (1968). Bystander intervention in emergencies: Diffusion of responsibility. *Journal of Personality and Social Psychology, 8*(4), 377–383.

Gansberg, M. (1964). 37 who saw murder didn't call the police. *New York Times:* http://www.nytimes.com/1964/03/27/37-who-saw-murder-didnt-call-the-police.html.

Graupmann, V., & Frey, D. (2014). Bad examples: How thinking about blind obedience can induce responsibility and courage. *Peace and Conflict: Journal of Peace Psychology, 20*(2), 124–134.

Kelly, B. (2003). *Worth repeating: More than 5,000 classic and contemporary quotes.* Grand Rapids, MI: Kregel.

Kinsella, E. L., Ritchie, T. D., & Igou, E. R. (2015). Zeroing in on heroes: A prototype analysis of hero features. *Journal of Personality and Social Psychology, 108*(1), 114–127.

Manning, R., Levine, M., & Collins, A. (2008). The legacy of the 38 witnesses and the importance of getting history right. *American Psychologist, 63*(6), 562–563.

Milgram, S. (1963). Behavioral study of obedience. *Journal of Abnormal and Social Psychology, 67*(4), 371–378.

Piff, P. K., Dietze, P., Feinberg, M., Stancato, D. M., & Keltner, D. (2015). Awe, the small self, and prosocial behavior. *Journal of Personality and Social Psychology, 108*(6), 883–899.

Seligman, M. E. P., Steen, T. A., Park, N., & Peterson, C. (2005). Positive psychology progress: Empirical validation of interventions. *American Psychologist, 60*(5), 410–421.

Sierksma, J., Thijs, J., & Verkuyten, M. (2014). With a little help from my friends: Bystander context and children's attitude toward peer helping. *Journal of Social Psychology, 154*(2), 142–154.

Zimbardo, P. (2008, September 23). TED Talk: The psychology of evil. https://www.youtube.com/watch?v=OsFEV35tWsg.

Notes

1. *Captain America: The First Avenger* (2011 motion picture).
2. Kelly (2003), p. 169.
3. *Captain America: The First Avenger* (2011 motion picture).
4. *Captain America Comics* #1 (1941).
5. Seligman et al. (2005).
6. Campbell (1949).
7. Campbell (1949).
8. *Captain America: The First Avenger* (2011 motion picture).

9. Graupmann & Frey (2014).
10. *Captain America: The First Avenger* (2011 motion picture).
11. Graupmann & Frey (2014), p. 126.
12. Milgram (1963).
13. Zimbardo (2008).
14. Zimbardo (2008).
15. *Captain America: The Winter Soldier* (2014 motion picture).
16. *Civil War* #1 (2006).
17. Piff et al. (2015)
18. *Iron Man* #275 (1991); *Tales of Suspense* #39 (1963); *Iron Man* (2008 motion picture).
19. *Iron Man* (2008 motion picture).
20. Seligman et al. (2005), p. 411.
21. *Iron Man* (2008 motion picture).
22. Darley & Latané (1968).
23. Gansberg (1964).
24. Manning et al. (2008).
25. *Captain America: The First Avenger* (2011 motion picture).
26. *The Avengers* (2012 motion picture).
27. *Captain America: The Winter Soldier* (2014 motion picture).

ID

TRAVIS LANGLEY

How mature does a hero have to be? There are many types of heroes, including those who have matured beyond purely infantile states of mind and even some who are prone to indulge in selfish, pleasure-seeking, primitive pursuits. Because Steve Rogers is more of the former and Tony Stark is more of the latter, Sigmund Freud might blame Mama Maria Stark for breast-feeding Tony too much . . . or not enough.

At the beginning of life, according to Freud, personality consists entirely of *id*: the inborn, instinctive self that will stay unconscious throughout life.[1] After the *ego* and the conscious mind develop (toward age 3—see Depth File II: Ego on page 102), the amoral id supposedly still exerts influence, and later it will compete with the influence of the moral *superego* as well (see Depth File III: Superego on page 148).[2] Freud said that the id operates on the *pleasure principle*, seeking immediate fulfillment of needs and desires.[3] An infant will need to learn to wait. An id-dominated adult tends not to wait.

A person with a *fixation*, as Freud originally used the term, is emotionally stuck (*fixated*) in an immature stage of personality development. People really do become emotionally stuck at certain points in life and can have difficulty moving on, perhaps because of trauma or for many other reasons.[4] Freud believed that unresolved issues keep a fixated individual from fully outgrowing that early stage. Some of an impetuous adult's behavior might suggest a degree of fixation in the infancy stage, which Freud called the *oral stage* because he considered the mouth to be the infant's primary source of achieving satisfaction (though sucking, crying, biting). An adult with an *oral fixation* would be more prone to expressing both joy and aggression through oral activities, as can be seen in Tony Stark's drinking and biting sarcasm.

What unresolved issues might cause an adult such as Tony to have developed an oral fixation? Freud attributed fixations to having needs met too little (frustration) or too much (over-indulgence). A person with lingering frustrations may ache unconsciously for those needs to be met—to get *closure*, so to speak—whereas an overindulged child may feel too comfortable to want to resolve issues and move forward. Maybe his mother, Maria Stark, ignored her child, or maybe she spoiled him. Spoiling would be easy to believe in light of the family's vast wealth and jet-setting lifestyle. Why blame an overcompensating mother more than an absent father? Blame Freud, who linked this stage strongly to the mother as the first person to whom a child connects and the person physically capable of breast-feeding. Weaning the child too early or too late supposedly raises the likelihood of an oral fixation. Scientifically speaking, one great flaw in Freud's approach is that he constructed his ideas so that there is no room for anyone to contradict him. They lacked *falsifiability*, or testability. Tony becomes an alcoholic?[5] Then he must not have been breast-fed enough, a Freudian might say. If information then indicates that he had been breast-fed well, then he must have been breast-fed too much and Freud must still be right according to Freud's own way of thinking. Whereas Freud saw his theory's resistance to contradiction as a good thing, his onetime colleague Carl Jung came to criticize it as being dogma instead of science.[6]

For a time, the comic book *Superior Iron Man* starred an id-driven Tony Stark. After a powerful telepath unleashes Tony's darker side, he becomes selfish, arrogant, and irresponsible. Driven by baser impulses but lacking ethics, he shows indifference to the concerns of others and also starts drinking again despite years of sobriety.[7] His aggressiveness, cynicism, and manipulativeness during this period match qualities Freud said manifest in individuals who become fixated later in infancy.[8]

Erik Erikson, a psychologist trained in the Freudian tradition by Sigmund's daughter Anna, recognized many of the same aspects of the way personality develops in stages, but with key differences. For one thing, he doubted that the id holds quite so much power over people. Erikson also focused on how social interactions shape personality (identifying *psychosocial* stages of personality development), as opposed to Freud's focus on body parts (*psychosexual* stages of development).[9] He, too, would have attributed Tony Stark's more infantile behavior to how well or poorly Maria Stark interacts with him and meets his needs. In the infancy stage, which Erikson referred to as *trust vs. mistrust* (sometimes *basic trust vs. mistrust*), Tony's mother apparently makes him less ready to trust individuals. Steve's mother, in contrast, teaches him to feel optimistic and to trust basic human nature, hence his later desire to trust individual superheroes to regulate themselves.

Regardless of controversy over his theories and shortage of empirical evidence to support many of his ideas, psychiatrist Sigmund Freud's views have affected both culture and popular perceptions of psychology and psychiatry. Freud's *psychodynamic (psychoanalytic)* approach is the best-known type of *depth psychology,* the collective term for areas that look *deep* into the unconscious to explain personality and actions. Whether or not he was correct when he said personality consists of id, ego, and superego, the concepts remain influential and offer an alternative way of comparing this book's featured superheroes because of the ways he claimed these parts of personality affect moral reasoning and decision making.

Comic Book References

Iron Man #128 (1979). "Demon in a Bottle." Script: D. Michelinie & B. Layton. Art: J. Romita Jr. & B. Layton.
Superior Iron Man #1–9 (2015). Scripts: T. Taylor. Art: Y. Çınar, F. Watanabe, R. Jose, J. Leisten, & W. Wong.

Other References

Buchen, L. (2012). Arrested development. *Nature, 484*(7394), 304–306.
Erikson, E. (1950). *Childhood and society.* New York, NY: Norton.
Erikson, E. (1959). Identity and the life cycle: Selected papers. *Psychological Issues, 1* (Monograph 1).
Erikson, E., & Erikson, J. (1989). *The life cycle completed* (extended version). New York, NY: Norton.
Freud, S. (1920). *Beyond the pleasure principle.* London, UK: Norton.
Freud, S. (1921). *Group psychology and ego-analysis.* Vienna, Switzerland: Internationaler Psychoanalytischer Verlag.
Freud, S. (1923/1927). *The ego and the id.* London, UK: Hogarth.
Freud, S., & Jung, C. G. (1974). *The Freud/Jung papers.* Princeton, NJ: Princeton University Press.
Kwon, P., & Olson, M. L. (2007). Rumination and depressive symptoms: Moderating role of defense style immaturity. *Personality and Individual Differences, 43*(4), 715-724.

Notes

1. Freud (1921).
2. Freud (1923/1927).
3. Freud (1920).
4. Buchen (2012); Kwon & Olson (2007).
5. *Iron Man* #128 (1979).
6. Freud & Jung (1974).
7. *Superior Iron Man* #1–9 (2015).
8. Freud (1920).
9. Erikson (1950, 1959); Erikson & Erikson (1989).

PART TWO

MISSIONS

Role models can inspire us in many ways. They can make us want to be better people without them even being real. This is especially true when they represent something greater than themselves, the ideals and values that strike deep within us all. A living person can also be a symbol.

CHAPTER FOUR

PUNCHING HITLER: SYMBOLS IN RED, WHITE, BLUE, AND GOLD

TOMMY CASH AND
TRAVIS LANGLEY

"Years ago, in simpler times, this suit and this shield were created as a symbol . . ."
—Captain America[1]

*"A symbol does not define or explain; it points beyond itself
to a meaning that is darkly divined yet still beyond our
grasp, and cannot be adequately expressed . . ."*
—psychiatrist Carl Jung[2]

What do we think of our heroes? Our views of heroes and heroism itself vary in ways that reflect our times and circumstances. The conflict between forces led by Captain America and Iron Man reflects differences in how we view both heroes and war itself during different eras. Cap embodies the hopes and ideals America carried into one war whereas Iron Man represents "all the things the hippies hated"[3] during a less popular conflict. Many other characters logically could have led the opposing superhero forces, but symbolically it had to be these two. Not only are they the most famous super-heroes to come out of twentieth-century wars, but also they each personify the different ideals that took America into each respective war—"framing the War on Terror through America's recent past."[4]

Despite the wealth of research on *altruism* (helping others at a cost or risk to oneself[5]) and our views on it, psychology has barely researched[6] the overlapping but more complex concept of *hero-ism* (prosocial behavior despite personal risk in a way that turns values and ideals into action[7]). The field does have a long history, however, of looking at symbols. A *symbol* represents something other than itself, whether concrete or abstract. Symbols hold power. Symbols help set the human race apart from all other species in this world. The leaders who quickly emerge during Marvel's Civil War each already symbolize the principles at the heart of their conflict, and their every interaction symbolizes the tumultuous relationship between the principles themselves.

Symbols

Deep Thoughts

Psychodynamic theorists analyze behavior and personality in terms of how conscious and unconscious mind interact. Sigmund Freud, Carl Jung, Alfred Adler, and others studied dreams and fiction for clues as to what might lie deep in the mind, believing unconscious contents leak into the conscious in the form of fantasy.[8] The fantasy's *manifest content* is the manifestation, what it's obviously about, and its *latent content* is the hidden part that reflects its deeper meaning. When Captain America and Iron Man argue, that manifest argument might contain layers of deeper meaning. Beyond the obvious representation of the clash between their ideologies, a Freudian might see their dispute as symbolizing the way the superego and id fight to control the mind's ego or—given that we are talking about Sigmund Freud, after all—masculine sexual competition.[9]

Pushing the Limit

Many storytellers deliberately weave symbolism into their tales, sometimes subtly burying symbols to influence unconsciously but at other times using obvious symbolism to achieve conscious effects. In the politically charged, multipart "Secret Empire" storyline published during the 1970s, Captain America fights the Secret Empire as an analogy for challenging corrupt behind-the-scenes activities among American politicians. The storyline ends with Cap finding out that the Secret Empire's villainous leader, "Number 1," is the U.S. president, who commits suicide rather than answer for his crimes.[10] The real-life Richard Nixon resigned in August of that year.[11]

The metaphors in Marvel's Civil War are strong as well: Readers caught on to the parallels between legislation that invaded privacy in the comic book world and the real-life USA PATRIOT Act, which had passed not long after the 9/11 tragedy. This meant fans with a conservative bent might be more likely to take the side of Iron Man, who was trying to keep everyone safe from future attacks, while more liberal-minded readers might choose Captain America, lover of liberty and freedom, who wasn't going to surrender to a wealthy arms dealer. This also paralleled the polarized political climate of the day, when much discourse seemed to boil down to the binary red state/blue state arguments.

Aspiration

During our second year of life, we begin showing advances in *representational ability*, the ability to represent objects and actions through symbols such as words and mental pictures, and we start to pretend.[12] Learning to interpret symbols is an essential childhood task. By age two, children demonstrate understanding that a picture represents something else.[13] After age three, we come to understand that eventually children become adults.[14] By age five, we imitate adults not only for immediate effect but also because adults represent what we can become. Heroes are no longer simply people who might save the day; they are people we might aspire to be. The child who colors a trash can lid to resemble Cap's shield[15] or who stands up to a mechanical monster while wearing a copy of another hero's mask[16] may feel empowered through identification with a superhero, as the symbols themselves convey a feeling of superpower.

To be fair to Iron Man, he is also an aspirational character. Steve Rogers may volunteer to become a superhero, but Tony Stark famously turns himself into one using scraps in a cave. As Stan Lee mentions in this book's foreword, he and his collaborators created Iron Man as the embodiment of what many readers hated at the time. Many were probably scared of going to Vietnam, and yet they adored Tony Stark, a rich arms dealer, partly because he had a literal and figurative change of heart.

Projection

The way we perceive fiction can sometimes say more about us than it says about the fiction itself. We see what we want to see, what *priming* (when triggering with one stimulus makes us more likely to notice related cues to or to interpret ambiguous stimuli as being related[17]) directs us to see, or what our *perceptual set* (each person's individual set of expectations regarding stimuli we are likely to encounter[18]) predisposes us to see. *Projective tests* present ambiguous stimuli like Rorschach inkblots in order to gain insight as to a test taker's personality or unconscious processes.[19] These tests are controversial because of concerns about psychodynamic assumptions, consistency in the way in which they're administered, and meaningfulness of their results.[20] Regardless of whether we can understand why one person says a cloud looks like a dancer while someone else insists it's a bunny, we know these differences can have meaning. Fearful individuals can perceive heights more extremely,[21] therapists can interpret ordinary actions as evidence supporting erroneous diagnoses,[22] and both left-wingers and right-wingers can interpret events in ways that reinforce their existing political attitudes.[23] If Captain America indeed is a symbol of America and people see America as different things, then the audience can project their own political ideologies onto the character.

Captain America's apparent assassination in *Civil War*'s aftermath stirred up a furor.[24] Suddenly, people who had not read a comic book in years—if ever—had opinions on why Captain America had died and on what issues America needed him to face instead of dying. At the time, the story's author observed, "What I found was that all the really hard-core, left-wing fans want Cap to be standing out on and giving speeches on the street corner against the Bush administration, and all the really right-wing [fans] all want him to be over in the streets of Baghdad, punching out Saddam."[25] Steve Englehart, who had pitted Cap against Richard Nixon[26] while writing Captain America's exploits in the 1970s, said that Captain America "stands for America as an ideal, not America as it's practiced."[27]

Inspiration

Fictional characters can inspire us in many ways as their stories cause us to feel specific emotions that can then motivate us.[28]

We mimic behavior we observe in others before we even learn to distinguish fact from fantasy, and this tendency does not simply disappear.[29] Because Captain America and Iron Man are fully human with no specific superpowers personally, with origins that make sense in terms of how our world operates, we can continue to see them as realistic role models even after the magical thinking of our preschool years begins to decline.[30] Even when we know that no radioactive spider or magic ring will give them superpowers, we can feel inspired by heroes— whether real or unreal—whose origins at least feel like they arise out of the rules of reality. Within the fiction, this real tendency to prefer more realistic role models as we grow might help account for why so many other superheroes more readily follow two who have no superpowers.

Meeting our heroes can be scary. What if they disappoint us? What if they judge us? We're often bursting to express the conflicting ways in which they have inspired us. Jessica Jones tells Captain America one reason why she gave up on being a superhero: "It became very clear that I could never be you. Any of you . . . I didn't have that thing that inspires people to be bigger than they are."[31] Sometimes we feel daunted by the idea of trying to live up to our heroes, but sometimes that motivates us even more. When people do brave things despite disadvantages, like the child in a third-world country who walks miles to get clean water for an infant sibling, they can inspire us to do more with what we have. According to Hercules, the mortal Captain America inspires the gods like that child can inspire us: "On Olympus, we measure wisdom against Athena, speed against Hermes, power against Zeus. But we measure courage against Captain America."[32]

Choosing Symbols, Choosing Sides

Red, white, and blue versus red and gold—the one color they share is red: Both have blood on them. They also have blood in them, which can symbolize their personal strengths. The leader who dresses in the American flag fights for liberty, while the leader who wears a machine the color of money (usually gold but occasionally silver) fights for a structured system. Neither side in the conflict needs to wave a banner because their leaders are their living emblems.

Both the audience and other characters in the Marvel Universe see Captain America as a symbol of America, but maybe a historic America, while Iron Man might represent modern America or corporate America.

Comic Book References

Alias #5 (2002). "Alias Investigations," part 5. Script: B. M. Bendis. Art: M. Gaydos.

Captain America #175 (1974). ". . . Before the Dawn!" Script: S. Englehart. Art: S. Buscema & V. Colletta.

Captain America #444 (1995). "Hope and Glory." Script: M. Waid. Art: R. Garney & M. Sellers.

Captain America #4 (2003). "The Extremists," part 1. Script: J. N. Rieber. Art: T. Hairsine & D. Miki.

Other References

Adler, A. (1927). *The practice and theory of individual psychology.* New York, NY: Harcourt, Brace, & World.

Bornstein, M. H., Haynes, O. M., O'Reilly, A. W., & Painter, K. (1996). Solitary and collaborative pretense play in early childhood: Sources of individual variation in the development of representational competence. *Child Development, 67*(6), 2910–2929.

Calhoun, B. (2011, July 19). *The politics of Captain America.* Salon: http://salon.com/2011/07/19/captain_america_politics.

Caparos, S., Fortier-St. Pierre, S., Gosselin, J., Blanchette, I., & Brisson, B. (2015). The tree to the left, the forest to the right: Political attitude and perceptual bias. *Cognition, 134,* 155–164.

DeLoache, J. S., Pierroutsakos, S. L., & Uttal, D. (2003). The origins of pictorial competence. *Current Directions in Psychological Science, 12*(4), 114–118.

Englehart, S. (n.d.). *Captain America II.* Steve Englehart Writes: http://www.steveenglehart.com/Comics/Captain America 20169-176.html.

Farsides, T., Pettman, D., & Tourle, L. (2013). Inspiring altruism: Reflecting on the personal relevance of emotionally evocative prosocial media characters. *Journal of Applied Social Psychology, 43*(11), 2251–2258.

Flavell, J. H. (2000). Development of children's knowledge about the mental world. *International Journal of Behavioral Development, 24*(1), 15–23.

Franco, Z. E., Blau, K., & Zimbardo, P. (2011). Heroism: A conceptual analysis and differentiation between heroic action and altruism. *Review of General Psychology, 15*(2), 99–113.

Freud, S. (1900/1965). *The interpretation of dreams.* New York, NY: Discus.

Freud, S. (1940). An outline of psychoanalysis. In *Standard edition of the complete works of Sigmund Freud* (vol. 23, pp. 141–207). London, UK: Hogarth.

Gustines, G. G. (2007, March 8). *Captain America is dead; national hero since 1941.* New York Times: http://www.nytimes.com/2007/03/08/books/08capt.html.

Haber, R. N. (1966). Nature on the effect of set on perception. *Psychological Review, 73*(4), 335–351.

Hero Construction Company (2015, January 21). *Philip Zimbardo and Matt Langdon at the Hero Round Table 2014.* https://www.youtube.com/watch?v=ujtkIaAfiSM.

Hunsley, J., & Mash, E. (2007). Evidence-based assessment. *Annual Review of Clinical Psychology, 3,* 29–51.

Jerit, J., & Barabas, J. (2012). Partisan perceptual bias and the information environment. *Journal of Politics, 74*(3), 672–684.

Jung, C. G. (1912). *Psychology of the unconscious.* London, UK: Kegan Paul.

Jung, C. G. (1926). Spirit and life. In G. Adler & R. F. C. Jull (Eds & trans.) *The collected works of C. G. Jung* (vol. 8, pp. 319–337). Princeton, NJ: Princeton University Press.

Kripal, J. J. (2011). *Mutants and mystics: Science fiction, superhero comics, and the paranormal.* Chicago, IL: University of Chicago Press.

Martin, C. L., Ruble, D. N., & Szkrybalo, J. (2002). Cognitive theories of early gender development. *Psychological, 128*(6), 903–933.

McClancy, K. (2015). Iron Curtain vs. Captain American exceptionalism: World War II and Cold War nostalgia in the Age of Terror. In K. M. Scott (Ed.), *Marvel Comics' Civil War and the Age of Terror* (pp. 108–119). Jefferson, NC: McFarland.

Morgan, D. (2007, March 7). *Captain America killed outside courthouse.* CBS News: http://www.cbsnews.com/news/captain-america-killed-outside-courthouse/.

Nelson, K. (2005). Evolution and development of human memory systems. In B. J. Ellis & D. F. Bjorklund (Eds.), *Origins of the social mind: Evolutionary psychology and child development* (pp. 319–345). New York, NY: Guilford.

Oatley, K. (2011). *Such stuff as dreams: The psychology of fiction.* West Sussex, UK: Wiley-Blackwell.

Piliavin, J. A., & Charng, H. (1990). Altruism: A review of recent theory and research. *Annual Review of Sociology, 16*(1), 27–65.

Porcelli, P. (2004). *Psychosomatic medicine and the Rorschach test.* Madrid, Spain: Psimatica.

Rachlin, H., & Locey, M. (2011). A behavioral analysis of altruism. *Behavioural Processes, 87*(1), 25–33.

Rakoczy, H., Tomasello, M., & Striano, T. (2004). Young children know that trying is not pretending: A test of the "behaving-as-if" construal of children's early concept of pretense. *Developmental Psychology, 40*(3), 388–399.

Robinson, B. (2007, March 8). *What the death of Captain America really means.* ABC News: http://abcnews.go.com/US/story?id=2934283.

Rosenhan, D. L. (1970). On being sane in insane places. *Science, 179,* 250–258.

Rothkopf, E. Z., & Billington, M. J. (1974). Indirect review of priming through questions. *Journal of Educational Psychology, 66*(5), 669–679.

Sacks, E. (2007, March 9). *Captain America croaks.* New York Daily News: nydailynews
.com/entertainment/music-arts/captain-america-killed-article-1.217626.
Seidler, V. J. (1989). *Rediscovering masculinity: Reason, language, and sexuality.* London,
UK: Routledge.
Teachman, B. A., Stefanucci, J. K., Clerkin, E. M., Cody, M. W., & Proffitt, D. R.
(2008). A new mode of fear expression: Perceptual bias in height fear. *Emotion, 8*(2),
296–301.
Woolley, J. D. (1997). Thinking about fantasy: Are children fundamentally different
thinkers and believer from adults? *Child Development, 68*(6), 991–1011.
Woolley, J. D., Phelps, K. E., Davis, D. L., & Mandell, D. J. (1999). Where theories
of mind meet magic: The development of children's beliefs about wishing. *Child
Development, 70*(3), 571–587.

Notes

1. *Captain America* #4 (2003).
2. Jung (1926), p. 336.
3. As Stan Lee told us in this book's foreword.
4. McClancy (2015), p. 108.
5. Farsides et al. (2013); Piliavin & Charng (1990); Rachlin & Locey (2011).
6. Hero Construction Company (2015).
7. Franco et al. (2011).
8. Freud (1900/1965); Jung (1912); Adler (1927).
9. Freud (1940); Seidler (1989).
10 *Captain America* #175 (1974).
11. Englehart (n.d.)
12. Bornstein et al. (1996).
13. DeLoache et al. (2003).
14. Martin et al. (2002).
15. *Captain America: The First Avenger* (2011 motion picture).
16. *Iron Man 2* (2010 motion picture); *The Amazing Spider-Man 2* (2014 motion
picture).
17. Rothkopft & Billington (1974).
18. Haber (1966).
19. Porcelli (2004).
20. Hunsley & Mash (2007).
21. Jerit & Barabas (2012); Teachman et al. (2008).
22. Rosenhan (1970).
23. Caparos et al. (2015).
24. Bonisteel (2007); Gustines (2007); Morgan (2007); Robinson (2007).
25. Sacks (2007).
26. *Captain America* #175 (1974).
27. Calhoun (2011).
28. Oatley (2011).
29. Flavell (2000); Nelson (2005); Rakoczy et al. (2004).
30. Woolley (1997); Woolley et al. (1999).
31. *Alias* #5 (2002).
32. *Captain America* #444 (1995)

The will to do good may not be enough. Power might not, either. Skill counts. After the origin, heroes face a steep learning curve if they hope to succeed and survive. I/O psychology can offer surprising insight by looking at the origin as a personnel matter and training in terms of human factors management. After all, heroes need efficiency, too.

CHAPTER FIVE

TRAINING TIME TALES WITH STEVEN AND ANTHONY: THE I/O PSYCHOLOGY OF GETTING BETTER AT BEING SUPER

TRAVIS LANGLEY AND E. PAUL ZEHR

"Look at Spider-Man, still haunted after all these years by the death of that girl he loved—Gwen. If he'd been properly trained, maybe he could have broken her fall without breaking her neck."
—Iron Man[1]

"Training is everything. The peach was once a bitter almond; cauliflower is nothing but cabbage with a college education."
—satirist Mark Twain[2]

Motivation, the drive to take action, is a powerful thing, but it may be insufficient without the *ability* to perform the action. Sheer motivation and physical ability do not a decathlon winner or concert pianist make. Similarly, before they become superheroes, Steve Rogers has motivation in abundance but is physically limited in his ability to stand up to bullies, whereas Tony Stark has gifts and resources aplenty but lacks the motivation to perform heroic acts. Different circumstances change Steve's physique and Tony's drive, but how do they learn the necessary skills to bring it all together? The same principles of *industrial/organizational (I/O) psychology* that help us better understand people in their occupations can offer clues as to what makes these men effective in their costumed activities.

How does someone become a career superhero? What abilities would such a person need to have? How resilient would each need to be, what other qualities will help someone keep going as a superhero, and what kind of training would be needed? Becoming a superhero is demanding enough. Remaining one would require even more work, dedication, and sacrifice.

Not all superheroes have day jobs. Even those who have "normal" employment—like Spider-Man, whose alter ego Peter Parker often works as a news photographer—tend to think of themselves as superheroes first. It is a bit like the teacher, waiter, or park ranger who says, "But I'm really a writer." They may not get paid to perform heroic feats, and yet superheroing becomes their *occupation*—the primary activity that occupies them. Major areas in I/O psychology (human factors, organizational psychology, and personnel psychology) could offer insight into the origins of Captain America and Iron Man and into key issues critical to their later conflict over whether superhumans should register with the government. While Steve Rogers sees superhero registration as a violation of liberties, Tony Stark looks upon registration as more of a *human resource management (HRM)* issue,[3] seeing superhumans who need to be managed.[4]

Function

Human factors professionals study the relationship between workers and things. This includes issues like workplace arrangement, equipment design, and human-machine interactions for the sake of improving satisfaction and efficiency overall. They focus on *ergonomics*, the science of work.[5] Superheroes could benefit from human factors pros' input on (among other things) costume design. They need outfits that are practical both physically and psychologically. Human factors research has, for example, helped improve the effectiveness of different types of gloves.[6] Imagine the Punisher dropping his bullets or Spider-Man fumbling to change web cartridges because of wearing the wrong glove. When Tony Stark configures his Iron Man suit to fire repulsor rays from his gloves instead of from something like his belt, he is making a human factors decision. So is the costume designer who shouts, "No capes!"[7]

Superhero costumes and even their accessories serve practical, task-related purposes and evoke particular reactions from others. Captain America's flag-themed outfit helps him inspire others, whereas the Punisher's black attire with the skull across his torso intimidates. Iron Man's costume—his exoskeletal suit of armor—inspires and motivates by exuding power and capability.

For a real Iron Man suit of armor to exist and to be applied usefully, it needs a kind of brain-machine interface that responds without conscious command.[8] The suit is often depicted as something that can be worn just like clothing—slip on, slip off. For it to work, it would be like clothing—except electronic clothing that connects directly to your brain and spinal cord. Such a suit must detect and respond to the millisecond timescale your nervous system works on. Simply responding to and amplifying movements would create too many delays—like having a live video conversation online. It would also be "smart clothing" with artificial intelligence functions and predictive learning that would help the suit anticipate scenarios, choices, and actions. In many ways the Iron Man suit of armor would be at once the best employee ever and a part of Tony's body, an ergonomic apparatus for completing his job successfully.

Organization

Organizational psychology investigates the relationship between employee and organization.[9] When they each become super-heroes, Steve Rogers and Tony Stark hold positions at opposite extremes in their organizational charts: Rogers gets recruited to be a buck private whose transformation promotes him to captain, whereas Stark inherits his company and adopts a super-hero identity that he initially claims is his own bodyguard. The recruit becomes a leader, and the leader acts as an employee.

Usually serving a consultant role, an organizational psychol-ogist will assess the organization's strengths and weaknesses in the course of assessing what the organization needs to do for the employees or (as with clubs and most super-teams) non-employee members. What kind of leader do they need? What should the organization do to foster communica-tion, motivation, and satisfaction? Information used to make these assessments may come from within the organization, perhaps by surveying employees. They may also come exter-nally from other organizations. When the government tries forming new superhero teams in every American state during the *Civil War* storyline, an organizational psychologist would likely advise them to take lessons from past super-teams: Why do the Avengers and X-Men endure in various forms,[10] why do the Defenders repeatedly break up for lengthy periods of time,[11] and why do the Champions quickly fall apart,[12] never to reunite? Learning such lessons might have helped many teams the government put together during its "50 State Initiative" keep going beyond the superheroes' Civil War.

People

I/O psychologists and other HRM professionals who are concerned with *personnel psychology* analyze the workers themselves. They work to improve methods of recruitment and selection, training, and evaluation. Act one of Captain America's origin is a story of recruitment and selection. Tony Stark selects, trains, and evaluates himself. Within his company, he generally leaves hiring decisions to people like Pepper Potts. Circumstances, not a careful review process, lead his friend Jim Rhodes to take over the Iron Man role in the comic books.[13] As either Iron Man or War Machine, Rhodes must work out how to be a superhero with little instruction from Stark.

Recruitment and Selection: Becoming Superhuman

Who is the right person for the job? There needs to be some kind of *person/position match* in which the one doing the job is suited for it. *Job analysis* (assessment of tasks to perform and competencies needed to perform them) lays the foundation for human resources activities. Even though Steve's commanding officer and the project's lead scientist both recognize the tasks their Super Soldier needs to become able to perform, their philosophies lead them to disagree on which strengths the first Super Soldier needs in order to perform them. Do they need the man who already has skills or the man with heart?

No one recruits Tony Stark to be Iron Man. He does not even set out to become a superhero. He's a man who builds a suit of armor with weapons to save his life. In the films, his journey from that to superhero takes longer. At first, he's out to stop the misuse of his own technology and happens to save villagers while he's at it. Having an epiphany, Tony Stark changes from being a capitalist industrial magnate solely concerned with fun and profit to becoming a founding member of the Avengers.

Training: Becoming Capable, Staying Competent

In action sequences, both Iron Man and Captain America move with certainty and a kind of aggressive and powerful grace. They are fully in control of themselves, their bodies, weapons, and the environment in which they are moving. That kind of athleticism and skill is typically the result of endless hours of hard work and training. This begs the question: How do Tony Stark and Steve Rogers get their training?

Captain America is an overall amazingly conditioned human and a fearless leader, but he has no superhuman powers. Instead, his abilities arise from a special "super-soldier serum" courtesy of Uncle Sam.[14] Real-life bioengineering of Captain America would involve a bit of pharmacology.[15]

Ampakines are drugs that improve learning, memory, attention, and alertness without the side-effects of other stimulants like caffeine and amphetamines. Ampakines facilitate the normal action of *glutamate*—the major excitatory neurotransmitter in the nervous system—to allow more ions into neurons and increase their activity. Ampakines basically boost this effect and may help lead to long lasting increases in transmission—a form of *neuroplasticity*, the ability for some nerves to take over the functions of other nerves. Essentially this is like a fuel additive that makes an engine run more efficiently and with more power output. But the engine is in your brain.

Another class of brain stimulants includes those that may change brain metabolism and brain structure. These include compound NSI-189. This compound may help with memory and cognition by stimulating stem cells found in the *hippocampus*—that major memory processing center deep inside your brain—to become functional neurons.

The First Avenger slings his shield at a distance, but his real forte is hand-to-hand fighting. He is constantly having knock-down-drag-out fights where he uses hitting, blocking, punching, and kicking with excellent skill. His training is army soldier circa WWII. This might bring to mind basic training, endless drilling, and practicing with weapons and empty hand fighting. Back in the early 1940s, training was much more ad hoc than training nowadays. In the Canadian army, for example, initial training was 30 days in the time after war was declared in 1939. This training time increased to three to four months in 1940 and 1941.[16] Yet this is still very short for the amount of time needed to acquire the skills we see Captain America put on view when fighting the Nazis, Hydra, A.I.M., or even street punks.

A lot of the training for WWII infantry involved exposure to the shock of combat so that successful actions could be carried out. When enemy fire was incoming, infantry soldiers were trained to go "down, crawl, observe, and fire." *Down* meant becoming a lesser target by immediately dropping to the ground. *Crawl* was an evasive movement to either find cover to protect from enemy fire or at least move away from the prior position so that the enemy might not know where to shoot. *Observe* meant to try and determine the location from which enemy fire was coming. The last, pretty logically, was *fire*—to shoot back. A major component of the training was the psychological resilience to maintain composure under extreme pressure.[17]

The Deadly Downside

To take the next step in a career, further training is often needed. In Captain America's case, he would be hampered by the era in which he initially trained in combat. Lack of training in the World War II–era American military had a deadly downside: More people were killed on the battlefield than in contemporary conflicts.

In order to progress as a superhero, Captain America would need more training at the initial and middle stages than Batman had, as Cap's instruction focuses on the fundamentals of hand-to-hand combat without sophisticated techniques from other cultures.[18] Cap would benefit from additional training in martial arts with striking, kicking, and joint locking, as well as projectile weapons, for a period of several years.[19] Quite a bit of training is needed to get his level of skill, and even more to fight but not kill.

Yet, in none of the timelines does Cap ever have more than a few months of training. So it's not really his fault that he winds up training on the job and using lethal force for a while during war. It's even worse for Tony Stark, who should seek training in both combat and flight.

To qualify as a jet fighter pilot, Tony would need extensive education and must be in top physical and psychological shape.[20] Once in flight school, Tony would spend hundreds of hours in classrooms and flight simulators. He would progress to advanced flight training where he would learn combat maneuvers and flying at night. This would take about five to seven years normally, but Tony is depicted as a man who can become an expert in a field overnight. In addition to combat as a kind of living jet fighter, Tony Stark as Iron Man also has many hand-to-hand fights as well. Perhaps he programs those skills into the computerized armor itself, but the information about those skills must originate from living combat experts.

Quite a bit of training is needed to be a safe and effective Iron Man or Captain America. The kind of movement skills that Tony and Steve use in their activities as Superheros are *procedural skills*. Those are skills that have a series of *discrete responses*—where there is a defined beginning and an end—connected together into elaborate sequences. Discrete skills, in contrast to continuous ones like running, are easy to forget.[21] Steve would have to rely more on *implicit memory*, drawing from previous experiences without consciously needing to think about them. Because Tony has his computerized suit to do so many things automatically, he does not have to rely as much on implicit memory.

Superhero Refresh Rate

I/O psychology can help us judge the efficacy of Steve Rogers and Tony Stark within their occupations as superheroes. Although the circumstances in their lives as Captain America and Iron Man provide them with the motivation and ability to become heroes, they also benefit from a host of other factors. They are performing their roles competently within their organizations, their inherent qualities make them good for the job, they delegate appropriately where necessary, and they are served well by ergonomic equipment.

However, these heroes cannot expect to maintain their skills just sitting around on a Quinjet or at Avengers Tower. The Okinawan karate master who pioneered the development of karate on the Japanese mainland, Gichin Funakoshi, wrote "Karate is like boiling water: Without heat, it returns to its tepid state."[22] This metaphor captures the underlying science of motor skill learning and retention that Captain America and Iron Man must heed in order to be successful and efficient heroes. So both Cap and Tony need refreshers on this at regular intervals. One suggestion? Seek the help of Daredevil for regular training. He did have the extreme training regimen needed—he's kind of a blind Batman, after all. And it's cheaper than installing an X-Men style Danger Room.

Comic Book References

Captain America Comics #1 (1941). "Meet Captain America." Script: Joe Simon. Art: Jack Kirby & Al Liederman.

Civil War #1 (2006). Script: M. Millar. Art: S. Nivens & D. Vines.

The Defenders #152 (1986). "The End of All Songs." Script: P. B. Gillis. Art: D. Perline & D. Barras.

Iron Man #170 (1983). "And Who Shall Clothe Himself in Iron?" Script: D. O'Neil. Art: L. McDonnell & S. Mitchell.

Iron Man/Captain America Casualties of War #1 (2007). "Rubicon." Script: C. N. Gage. Art: J. Haun & M. Morales.

The Spectacular Spider-Man #17 (1978). "Whatever happened to the Iceman?" Script: B. Mantlo. Art: S. Buscema & D. Hunt.

Other References

Aamodt, M. G. (2013). *Industrial/organizationl psychology: An applied approach* (7th ed.). Belmont, CA: Wadsworth.

Coswill, A. (2015). *Marvel—The Avengers: Ultimate character guide.* New York, NY: DK.

Dianat, L., Haslegrave, C. M., & Stedmon, A. W. (2010). Short and longer direction effects of protective gloves on hand performance capabilities and subjective assessments in a screw-driving task. *Ergonomics, 53*(12), 1468–1483.

Funakoshi, G. (1975). *Karate-do: My way of life.* Tokyo, Japan: Kodansha.

Hogg, I. V., & Chappell, M. (1989, August-September). Bren gunners, NW Europe, 1944–45. *Military illustrated: Past and present magazine, 20*, 10–20.

Mallory, M. (2014). *X-Men: The characters and their universe.* New York, NY: Marvel.

Mathis, R. L., Jackson, J. H., & Valentine, S. R. (2013). *Human resource management* (14th ed.). Boston, MA: Cengage.

McCauley-Bush, P. (2011). *Ergonomics: Foundational principles, applications, and technologies.* Boca Raton, FL: CRC.

Nelson, J. B., & Mital, A. (1995). An ergonomic evaluation of dexterity and tactility with increase in examination/surgical glove thickness. *Ergonomics, 38*(4), 723–733.

Salvendy, G. (2012). *Handbook of human factors and ergonomics* (4th ed.). New York, NY: Wiley.

Shih, Y., & Wang, M. J. (1997). The influence of gloves during maximum volitional torque exertion of supination. *Ergonomics, 40*(4), 465–475.

Stacey, C. P. (1948). *The Canadian Army 1939–1945.* Ottawa, Canada: King's Printer.

Twain, M. (1894). *The tragedy of Pudd'nhead Wilson.* New York, NY: Charles L. Webster.

U. S. Air Force ROTC. (n.d.) *Preparing for a flight career.* USAF ROTC: https://www.afrotc.com/college-life/flight.

Willms, K., Wells, R., & Carnahan, H. (2009). Glove attributes and their contribution to force decrement and increased effort in power grip. *Human Factors, 51*(6), 797–812.

Zehr, E. P. (2008). *Becoming Batman: The possibility of a hero.* Baltimore, MD: Johns Hopkins.

Zehr, E. P. (2011). *Inventing Iron Man.* Baltimore, MD: Johns Hopkins.

Zehr, E. P. (2014). *Out of the deep freeze: Captain America, the Winter Soldier, and the wood frog.* Scientific American: http://blogs.scientificamerican.com/guest-blog/out-of-the-deep-freeze-captain-america-the-winter-soldier-and-the-wood-frog/.

Notes

1. *Iron Man/Captain America: Casualties of War* #1 (2007).
2. Twain (1894).
3. Mathis et al. (2013).
4. *Civil War* #1 (2006).
5. McCauley-Bush (2011).
6. Dianat et al. (2010); Nelson & Mital (1995); Shih & Wang (1997); Willms et al. (2009).
7. *The Incredibles* (2004 motion picture).
8. Zehr (2011).
9. Aamodt (2013).
10. Coswill (2015); Mallory (2014).
11. e.g., *The Defenders* #152 (1986).
12. *The Spectacular Spider-Man* #17 (1978).
13. *Iron Man* #170 (1983).
14. *Captain America Comics* #1 (1941).
15. Zehr (2014).
16. Stacey (1948).
17. Hogg & Chappell (1989).
18. Zehr (2008).
19. Zehr (2008).
20. U. S. Air Force ROTC (n.d.).
21. Zehr (2008).
22. Funakoshi (1975).

Expectations for how people act based on gender may arise for social, physical, environmental, or other reasons. Regardless of why gender roles exist, they exert a powerful influence on many people. "Real men" risk following unwritten scripts—social norms for how they ought to act. When well-trained heroes symbolize patriotic values and steely manliness, is conflict inevitable?

CHAPTER SIX

CODES OF MASCULINITY: THE ROAD TO CONFLICT

ALAN KISTLER AND BILLY SAN JUAN

"The code of masculinity requires that men be aggressive, dominant, achievement oriented, self-sufficient, adventure seeking, and emotionally restricted and that they avoid all things feminine, characteristics that both take a toll on men's mental health . . ."
—psychologist Ronald F. Levant[1]

"Apparently I'm volatile, self-obsessed, and don't play well with others"
—Tony Stark[2]

Men often adhere to social norms for masculinity and the values that come with it. Some theories posit that these norms are socially learned, while other theories posit a less unidirectional view and suggest a series of micro and macro social factors.[3] Many of these masculine values can be seen during the events of the crossover story *Civil War*, in which Iron Man and Captain America find themselves in conflict due to their opposing opinions on the morality and legality of the Superhuman Registration Act. Four themes of masculinity provide a framework to see the factors at play that may exacerbate that conflict and to help us understand the uncharacteristic clash between America's iron-clad, high-tech hero and America's shield-toting, value-driven soldier.

Dimensions of Masculinity

The array of traits and characteristics socially expected in men as a gender, known as *masculinity,* is a topic that is examined through many different lenses in the psychology world. The literature provides a plethora of paradigms ranging from psychodynamic and social learning to psychophysiological and gender role strain.[4] These paradigms are based in different views on psychology, but all have one thing in common: They seek to explain the inner workings of a person.

Themes of Masculinity

Four themes offer a definition of the socialized construct known as masculinity.[5]

No Sissy Stuff

In many cultures, masculinity is defined as the strong opposite of femininity.[6] Men are often socialized to believe that behaviors, thoughts, and expressions of feelings, traditionally attributed to women, are signs of weakness. If a young boy is hurt on a playground and cries, peers may mock him by saying he's "crying like a girl." If men aren't athletically gifted, others may say they "throw like a girl." When women represent vulnerability, any manifestation of vulnerability may be punished socially by peers.

Tony Stark regularly engages in surface-level romances, allowing for physical intimacy but rarely true emotional connection. He is promiscuous and portrays the gender role ideal of sexual dominance, often treating women as mere sex objects.[7] He refuses to express to others the weakness he feels over having a heart condition and, in his early comics, keeps the truth of his health a secret from his assistant, Virginia "Pepper" Potts, whom he loves.[8] The events that lead to him becoming Iron Man also involve traumatic experiences that include being attacked by terrorists, waking up to find that he is their captive, dealing with a life-threatening injury, being unable to prevent the death of his friend and fellow captive, and using lethal force on other human beings during his escape immediately afterward.[9]

All of this happens within just a couple of days, yet Tony does not seek counseling after returning home. Instead, he dives into a new life of violence by using increasingly advanced Iron Man suits to combat supervillains and terrorists. The violence, though novel to his party lifestyle, plays into deep-rooted social norms for violence regulated by traditional masculinity roles.[10]

> *"Nobody can help me! Nobody can repair my damaged heart! Nobody can guarantee how much longer it will keep beating! Nobody can ever know the torment felt by Iron Man!"*
> —Tony Stark[11]

In contrast to Stark, young Steve Rogers is a sensitive idealist who wears his heart on his sleeve. He opposes bullies without buying into the masculinity narrative that violence or the death of an enemy are positive goals. The super-soldier serum and "vita-rays" that make him a super-soldier vastly increase his physical attributes and muscle mass, and his many battles toughen him up emotionally, but he never loses touch with his original feelings. Even years later, he is open about his doubts and fears to his friends[12] despite his role as leader and, during the end of *Civil War*, does not hide his tears when he concludes the conflict cannot be won.[13]

Be the Big Wheel

A slightly outdated metaphor, the "Big Wheel," is the idea that masculinity is established though success, power, wealth, and fame.[14] Such things support antiquated notions that a man is to be the "breadwinner" of the home and the "head of the house." A person's masculinity is measured in accomplishments and achievements that are obvious to outside observers and often involve some competition with others, taking a slot only available to one person or a small group deemed worthy. In competitive sports, the framework is laid so that we have a "first place," an "MVP," and a "Hall of Fame."

Iron Man immediately installs himself as leader of the Avengers when that team forms, perhaps because it seems the obvious place for him.[15] Of the original team members, Tony Stark is the wealthiest, the most popular and famous in the public eye, arguably the most scientifically proficient, and the only member to also lead an international conglomerate (being the CEO of Stark Industries). These traits are seen as highly masculine in a patriarchal society: He is rich, he is smart, and he is powerful. Even after officially turning over leadership of the Avengers to Captain America, Tony often acts like the others should naturally take his lead when he has a plan. Tony later reveals that such behavior is partially because he feels inadequate compared to Steve, despite his own achievements, and is over-compensating.[16]

> Tony Stark: "Everyone feels inadequate next to you. God knows I always have . . . ."[17]

Having grown up a poor person often regarded as a weakling, Steve Rogers is aware that people can have a lot to offer despite not having obvious accomplishments or being highly regarded by others, leading him to welcome heroes such as Spider-Man into the Avengers even when others wonder if the strange and often goofy-acting adventurer is a proper fit for the team.[18] However, Cap still adheres to the Big Wheel idea, wanting to be seen as "the big guy." He often stresses the need for regular combat training and exercises to his teammates, whatever their level of power or experience may be, since his days in the military and life on literal battlefields have taught him that such things are necessary to be an accomplished person. Military masculinity often involves such rituals.

The Sturdy Oak

To anyone who sees masculinity as relying on the values of logical thinking, toughness, and independence, men are not allowed to show emotion, admit any sort of weakness, or panic even in extreme situations. To see examples of this, we need only look at the majority of leaders we have in patriarchal systems. Despite the sex of the leader, they are idealized and judged by these characteristics. They are expected to be headstrong and resolved, to never surrender, to keep calm and remain steadfast, and not to act emotionally.[19]

As Tony Stark grows older, he becomes more aware of his vulnerability even if he won't admit it to most other people, such as when he drunkenly makes a rescue attempt that actually endangers lives, an event that forces him to face his alcoholism.[20] However, his actions sometimes contradict this more mature attitude toward accountability. He argues that the Superhuman Registration Act will bring about a system based on trust and transparency yet he manipulates friends and colleagues—for example, programming the armor he gifts to Spider-Man with secret controls allowing him to disable and control the web-slinger if he deems it necessary.[21]

Captain America openly admits fears and doubts to trusted friends, but he also becomes more guarded about seeming flawed in front of those who clearly see him as an inspiration. This plays into the idea that weakness is unacceptable for a man to display, that fear and doubt are manifestations of vulnerability.[22] When he is asked by members of the public to run for president, he refuses on the basis that he is meant to represent American ideals and not specific American beliefs, which is partially true while also a convenient way of avoiding being seen as a human being rather than as a living symbol.[23] Indeed, as soon as it is realized the super-soldier serum that created him cannot be perfectly duplicated, the military tells Steve that he needs to be a symbol rather than merely another soldier, and he evidently never forgets that.[24]

Give 'Em Hell

Masculinity values aggression and risk-taking. Men are socialized to "go for it," "throw caution to the wind," and "rebel." Any traditional hero's tale will provide proof that men are socialized to be forceful heroes, using strength to conquer any obstacle. It is dichotomous: Either you are the victor or you are the loser.

Steve Rogers becomes Captain America in order to serve the American government, but after encountering various corrupt and misguided officials, as well as spies, he no longer accepts that authority figures are automatically in the right.[25] When

he feels he is in direct opposition to the government, he sometimes takes on new identities to symbolize his rebellion, such as
Nomad,[26] the Captain,[27] and the Ex-Patriot,[28] but he does not
do so during *Civil War*, perhaps to symbolize that the problem
is not just a difference of opinion but that the Superhuman
Registration Act is un-American.

Although characters such as Steve Rogers might embrace
masculinity narratives and gender expectations less fervently
than Tony Stark, Steven Rogers does not escape them entirely
due to how steeped they are in the culture in which he was
brought up. That Tony and Steve are both following such
expectations, including the idea that one must fight rather than
talk about differences, adds to the tragedy of their conflict, as
they are both willingly falling prey to flawed values, which leads
them to sacrifice some of their own principles in the process.

Masculinity and Violence

Men are historically stereotyped per ideals congruent with
masculinity. Men are more often seen as dominant and assertive
and also as potentially violent.[29] An examination of the values
men are often socialized to embody can help explain factors in
how the Superhuman Registration Act became a war.

Values for Violence

> *"As a man matures, he becomes increasingly capable*
> *of providing his own inhibitors and of resisting the*
> *encouragement to act aggressively."*
> —psychologist Christopher Kilmartin[30]

Many influences, including personal values, shape the processes
that allow men to act in an aggressive manner toward others.[31]
These values do not doom man to act as a mindless barbarian

nor reduce the male sex to animalistic grunts and primitive desires. Instead, they provide insight into the psychological mechanisms that may play a role in why the civil war occurs.

- *Separation of self from others*: It is easier to destroy the enemy if you view the enemy without the lens of empathy. Tony and Steve distance themselves from their mutual understandings and friendship, arguing that such things have to be set aside for the greater good.
- *Objectification of others*: This refers to seeing others not as human beings, but rather as objects. This value shows how two friends such as Tony and Steve can view each other not as humans, colleagues, or heroes, but rather as the enemy.
- *Externalization of issues*: Men are often ingrained with the notion that emotions are to be coped with through external means such as exercise, alcohol, or violence. Likewise, many are trained to believe that issues stem from the outside world rather than internal mechanisms. Neither Steve nor Tony takes much time to consider losses or how the conflict continues to escalate, choosing instead to lose themselves in work and to plan their next moves.
- *Overattention to tasks*: In many cases, men value tasks and task completion. Oftentimes, this overattention to a task can lead to logical mistakes. An example of this occurs when violence or manipulation is used to help someone, only to have these methods hurt the person in the end. On a global scale, war can be seen in this manner. We kill other humans in order to protect human life. Tony wants to end the conflict as quickly as possible and agrees to recruit supervillains known for being untrustworthy and using lethal methods. Steve

gathers supporters on the basis that they can't trust the
government not to be manipulative or to use ethical
tactics; but he then goes on to employ manipulation
himself by using spies to infiltrate Tony's side.

- *Reinforcement*: Reinforcement by means of rewards for
  traditionally masculine roles occurs often. The reward
  does not necessarily need to be tangible. In many cases,
  the reward is social or emotional in nature. Respect,
  responsibility, and honor are three of the many ways
  a certain type of behavior can be rewarded. In *Civil
  War*, a victory is reinforced by that side's emotional
  satisfaction that their philosophy is triumphing.
  Before the Stamford Incident that sparks off *Civil War*,
  Tony Stark is haunted by making a fool of himself at
  the United Nations and having to resign his post as
  Secretary of Defense.[32] By his actions during *Civil War*,
  he regains government trust and even the respect of a
  woman who lost her son in the Stamford Incident and
  had considered Iron Man to be partly responsible.

- *Violent role models*: Very few poets, dancers, and
  artists serve as role models for men. Rather, men are
  socialized at a young age to idolize and emulate men
  who are violent and strong. Steve is a product of
  military culture during a wartime era. Tony is a product
  of industrial culture parallel to war, and his father is a
  war profiteer who makes much of his wealth through
  military contracts.

- *Drug use*: Drug use is a large factor in violence due to
  reducing the inhibition toward violence. Tony Stark
  periodically has difficulties as a result of alcohol abuse
  and addiction, such as when he uses his armor while
  drunk and puts lives in danger.[33] He later tells Captain
  America that his personal experience with losing

control has convinced him that any superhero could endanger innocents and that measures need to be taken to prevent this.[34]

- *Social acceptance*: It is socially acceptable for men to be aggressive or violent. Both leaders of *Civil War* are expected to perform as military generals for their sides. As such, they are socially likely to perform in a congruent manner. Both Tony and Steve can be seen as being uncharacteristically aggressive and unwilling to debate strategy, but both justify this as a by-product of their new roles and conflict.

- *Low masculine self-esteem*: Low masculine self-esteem, or uncertainty of one's identity or status, may lead to violent behavior. A push–pull tendency occurs wherein a person who feels less in control may attempt to regain it by frantic means. Relatedly, males in patriarchal societies are often taught that their value lies not in their inherent being but rather by their works. Steve and Tony each believe the other is still a good person and so they doubt themselves at times, but each then continues the battle based on the fact that the other's actions must come to a halt.

- *Peer support and "urging on"*: Peer support is a large factor in determining if violence is encouraged. Peers, such as those found on either side of Tony and Steve's conflict, reinforce their philosophies about the appropriateness of violence. During *Civil War*, Spider-Man regularly asks Iron Man and others if they're pursuing their goals in the best way or if they've forgotten their principles. Likewise, Nighthawk asks Captain America more than once if he's taking into account the damage that his rebellion causes.

Our Own Worst Enemy

Men are trained for war. Stereotypes of masculinity are ingrained at an early age and grow with time. Men are socialized to value strength over vulnerability, status over cooperation, stoicism over emotion, and punishment over kindness—not every individual man, to be sure, but men on average, as a population, as a gender role norm[35] whether it works well or not in this day and age. Only when Captain America displays more insight into the mechanisms driving their actions and the repercussions on their conflict does he end the superhero civil war. Perhaps if they question the forces that define the Man in Iron Man and the Captain in Captain America, they can be more complete as individuals and more capable of saving the world.

Comic Book References

Adventures of Captain America #1 (1991). "First Flight of the Eagle." Script: F. Nicieza. Art: K. Maguire, J. Rubenstein, & T. Christopher.

Adventures of Captain America #2 (1991). "Betrayed by Agent X." Script: F. Nicieza. Art: K. Maguire & T. Austin.

Avengers #1 (1963). "The Coming of the Avengers!" Script: S. Lee. Art: J. Kirby & D. Ayers.

Avengers #2 (1963). "The Space Phantom." Script: S. Lee. Art: J. Kirby & P. Reinman.

Avengers #500–501 (2004). "Avengers Disassembled," parts 1–2. Script: B M. Bendis. Art: D. Finch & D. Miki.

Captain America #176 (1974). "Captain America Must Die!" Script: S. Englehart. Art: S. Buscema & V. Colletta.

Captain America #180 (1974). "The Coming of the Nomad." Script: S. Englehart. Art: S. Buscema & V. Colletta.

Captain America #250 (1980). "Cap for President!" Script: R. Stern, D. Perlin, R. McKenzie, & J. Shooter. Art: J. Byrne & E. Hannigan.

Captain America #336. (1987). "Natural Calling." Script: M. Gruenwald. Art: T. Morgan & D. Hunt.

Captain America #451 (1996). "Plan A." Script: M. Waid. Art: R. Garney & S. Koblish.

Civil War #5 (2006). Script: M. Millar. Art: S. McNiven, D. Vines, M. Morales, J. Dell & T. Townsend.

Civil War #7 (2007, February). Script: M. Millar. Art: S. McNiven, D. Vines, M. Hollowell, & C. Eliopoulos.

Civil War: The Confession (2007). Script: B. M. Bendis. Art: A. Maleev.

Iron Man/Captain America: Casualties of War #1 (2007). Script: C. N. Gage. Art: J. Haun & M. Morales.

Iron Man #124 (1979). "Pieces of Hate." Script: D. Michelinie. Art: J. Romita Jr., B. Layton, B. McLeod, & B. Wiacek.

Iron Man #125 (1979). "The Monaco Prelude." Script: D. Michelinie. Art: J. Romita Jr. & B. Layton.

Iron Man #126 (1979). "The Hammer Strikes!" Script: D. Michelinie. Art: J. Romita Jr. & B. Layton.

Iron Man #127 (1979). "A Man's Home Is His Battlefield . . ." Script: D. Michelinie. Art: J. Romita Jr. & B. Layton.

Iron Man #128 (1979). "Demon in a Bottle." Script: D. Michelinie & B. Layton. Art: J. Romita Jr. & B. Layton.

Iron Man #225–231 (1988). "Stark Wars." Script: D. Michelinie & B Layton. Art: M. Bright & B. Layton.

New Avengers #1 (2005). "Breakout," part 1. Script: B. M. Bendis. Art: D. Finch & D. Miki.

Tales of Suspense #39 (1963). "Iron Man Is Born!" Script: S. Lee. Art. D. Heck.

Tales of Suspense #54 (1964). "The Mandarin's Revenge!" Script: S. Lee. Art: D. Heck.

Tales of Suspense 57 (1964). "Hawkeye, the Marksman!" Script: S. Lee. Art: D. Heck.

Other References

Addis, M., Reigeluth, C., & Schwab, J. (2016). Social norms, social construction, and the psychology of men and masculinity. In Y. J. Wong & S. R. Wester (Eds.), *APA handbook of men and masculinities* (pp. 81–104). Washington, DC: American Psychological Association.

Bem, S. L. (1981). Gender schema theory: A cognitive account of sex typing. *Psychological Review, 88*(4), 354–364.

Berger, J. M. (2005). Impact of gender role conflict: Traditional masculine ideology, alexithymia, and age on men's attitudes toward psychological help seeking. *Psychology of Men and Masculinity, 6*(1), 73–78.

Berke, D. S., Wilson, L., Mouilso, E., Speir, Z., & Zeichner, A. (2015). *Sex Roles, 72*(11–12), 509–520.

Brannon, R. (1985). Dimensions of the male sex role in America. In A. G. Sargent (Ed.), *Beyond sex roles* (pp. 296–316). New York, NY: West.

Diamond, M. J. (2015). The elusiveness of masculinity: Primordial vulnerability, lack, and the challenges of male development. *Psychoanalytic Quarterly, 84*(1), 47–102.

Graef, S. T., Tokar, D. M., & Kaut, K. P. (2010). Relations of masculinity ideology, conformity to masculine role norms, and masculine gender role conflict to men's attitudes toward and willingness to seek career counseling. *Personality of Men and Masculinity, 11*(4), 319–333.

Kilmartin, K. (2010). *The masculine self* (4th ed.). Cornwall-on-Hudson, NY: Sloan.

Levant, R. (2006). Foreword. In Englar-Carlson, M. & Stevens, M. (Eds.), *In the room with men: A casebook of therapeutic change* (pp. xv–xx). Washington, DC: American Psychological Association.

Levant, R. & Richmond, K. (2016). The gender role strain paradigm and masculine ideologies. In Y. J. Wong & S. R. Wester (Eds.), *APA handbook of men and masculinities* (pp. 23–49). Washington, DC: American Psychological Association.

Murray, G., Judd, F., Jackson, H., Fraser, C., Komiti, A., Pattison, P., Wearing, A., & Robins, G. (2008). Big boys don't cry: An investigation of stoicism and its mental health outcomes. *Personality and Individual Differences, 44*(6), 1369–1381.

Nobis, R., & Sanden, I. (2008). Young men's health: A balance between self-reliance and vulnerability in the light of hegemonic masculinity. *Contemporary Nurse, 29*(2), 205–217.

Steinberg, M., & Diekman, A. B. (2016). The double-edged sword of stereotypes of men. In Y. J. Wong & S. R. Wester (Eds.), *APA handbook of men and masculinities* (pp. 433-456). Washington, DC: American Psychological Association.

Thomas, P. (1996). Big boys don't cry? Mental health and the politics of gender. *Journal of Mental Health, 5*(2), 107–110.

White, A. (2009). Big boys really don't cry: Considering men's reluctance to engage in counseling. *Counselling Psychology Review, 24*(3–4), 2–8.

Notes

1. Levant (2006), pp. xvii–xviii.
2. *The Avengers* (2012 motion picture).
3. Addis et al. (2016).
4. Levant & Richmond (2016).
5. Brannon (1985).
6. Kilmartin (2010).
7. Kilmartin (2010).
8. *Tales of Suspense* #57 (1964).
9. *Tales of Suspense* #39 (1963).
10. Kilmartin (2010).
11. *Tales of Suspense* #54 (1964).
12. *Adventures of Captain America* #1 (1991).
13. *Civil War* #7 (2007).
14. Brannon (1985).
15. *Avengers* #1–2 (1963).
16. *Iron Man/Captain America: Casualties of War* #1 (2007).
17. *Civil War: Casualties of War* (2006).
18. *New Avengers* #1 (2005).
19. Graef et al. (2010); Murray et al. (2008); Thomas (1996). White (2009).
20. *Iron Man* #128 (1979).
21. *Civil War* #5 (2006).
22. Diamond (2015); Nobis & Sanden (2008).
23. *Captain America* #250 (1980).
24. *Adventures of Captain America* #2 (1991).
25. *Captain America* #176 (1974).
26. *Captain America* #180 (1974).
27. *Captain America* #336 (1987).
28. *Captain America* #451 (1996).
29. Steinberg & Diekman (2016).
30. Kilmartin (2010).
31. Kilmartin (2010).
32. *Avengers* #500–501 (2004).
33. *Iron Man* #128 (1979); *Avengers* #500–501 (2004).
34. *Iron Man/Captain America: Casualties of War* #1 (2007).
35. Bem (1981); Berger (2005); Berke (2015).

Many kinds of intelligence exist. No IQ test can measure them all. What does it even mean to be "the smartest man in the room"? If we're trying to guess how well a so-called supergenius might fare against a master of combat strategy as the two combatants lead their forces on a field a battle, we might learn a lesson or two from a game where the sides really are black and white.

CHAPTER SEVEN

DEFEATING THE GENIUS: GENERAL INTELLIGENCE VS. SPECIFIC ABILITY

MARTIN LLOYD

"An intelligence agency that fears intelligence? Historically, not awesome."
—Tony Stark[1]

> *"Excelling at chess has long been considered a symbol*
> *of more general intelligence. That is an incorrect*
> *assumption in my view, as pleasant as it might be."*
> —chess Grandmaster Garry Kasparov[2]

The evaluation of intelligence from a psychological perspective is more complicated than it may seem on a surface level. Intelligence encompasses a variety of cognitive abilities, which, generally speaking, are those abilities necessary for survival and advancement within a given culture.[3] That said, there are different kinds of intelligence. Tony Stark (Iron Man) appears to be one of the most overall intellectually gifted characters in the Marvel Universe. The many suits of armor created with his considerable intellect are adaptable and grant him physical prowess far in excess of even stronger-than-human characters like Steve Rogers (Captain America). Tony is highly adept at using technology to solve nearly any problem. These various abilities suggest Tony has a high level of generalized intellectual ability, referred to as *Spearman's g*, or simply *g*.[4] Steve's many achievements also suggest someone of high-average to superior intellectual ability; he is simply not an outlier on the intellectual bell curve like Tony. Steve does have one incredibly well-developed intellectual ability, however; he is an amazing strategic thinker, indicating a well-developed specific intellectual ability. Is this one ability sufficient to overcome Tony's various gifts, allowing the strategic thinker to defeat a genius? How can someone be a better strategist than a more intelligent opponent?

What Is Intelligence?

Clinically speaking, intelligence is defined simply by performance on a standardized intelligence test, or IQ test, relative to the established norms for one's age group. At present, the most commonly used IQ tests are the various Wechsler Intelligence Scales. These tests set the average IQ for the population at 100. Practically speaking, about two-thirds of the population have IQs in the middle of the range, between 85 and 115.[5] The score of 130 marks the low end of what is typically termed the *Very Superior* or "gifted" range, and less than 3% of the population would receive a score this high or higher.

Looking at intelligence as a score on a test says relatively little about what is actually being measured. Intelligence has often been conceptualized as drawing on one basic ability. This means that all intellectual tasks use some degree of this general ability, which explains why various subtests of intelligence, each measuring different abilities, tend to be correlated with one another (e.g., someone with a high score on one ability tends to have high scores on others). In addition to g, there are also more specific factors that contribute to intelligence. Among these are crystallized and fluid intelligence, where *crystallized intelligence* (typically measured by tests of verbal ability) is a measure of learning and *fluid intelligence* (typically measured by performance tasks and measures of visuospatial ability) is roughly equivalent to problem-solving ability.[6]

General intelligence, or g, is measured by assessing a variety of specific abilities thought to tap into some degree of the general factor. While these specific abilities seem to be associated with g, the relationship is not the same at every level of intellectual ability. In fact, specific abilities seem to correlate more with IQ at lower levels of intellectual ability than they do at higher levels.[7] Typically, individuals with high IQs tend to show a greater discrepancy between crystallized and fluid abilities than do those with normal or low IQs, generally with high crystallized intelligence but variable fluid intelligence.[8] Tony would seem to be an exception to this. His mechanical aptitude suggests a high degree of performance ability or fluid intelligence. He is also well-educated and verbally facile. That is, he is able to use verbal skills to high advantage, as evident in his success in business and politics (e.g., being appointed Secretary of Defense[9]). Therefore, he also demonstrates a high degree of crystallized ability. There do not appear to be any specific intellectual abilities in which Tony is notably deficient. Thus, he demonstrates high levels of various specific abilities and also a high level of general intelligence, likely several standard deviations even above the Superior range, making him a very formidable opponent.

Steve Rogers and the Game of Chess

Steve may not be Tony's equal in terms of general intellectual ability, but he is a world-class (and perhaps universal-class) strategist. During one universal crisis, Steve and the other Avengers aid a group of aliens. While the human contingent is largely ignored by the Shi'ar and other "advanced" races, Steve ultimately devises the plan that gives them their first victory.[10] From this point on, the alien races defer to him in matters of strategy. Therefore, despite perhaps lacking the breadth of Tony's overall intellectual abilities, Steve is still a master strategist. There is, unsurprisingly, little research on the cognitive abilities of World War II–era super-soldiers who have repeatedly saved the world. Looking for an analog, however, we can see that Steve often succeeds in battle, especially when acting in a leadership capacity, by putting the right performers where they can do the most good and by anticipating his opponents' moves. These actions are not unlike those actions typically undertaken by chess players. Given his success as a strategist, Steve would seem to be equivalent to a chess grandmaster, except that he is acting in combat situations throughout the Marvel Universe instead of on a game board. While there may be no research on super-soldiers, plenty has been said about chess players.

Unlike someone like Tony, who seems to have a high IQ level underlying a variety of well-developed abilities, expert chess players can show significant discrepancies between fluid and crystallized intelligence. Groups of expert chess players have demonstrated an average *Performance IQ* (i.e., an overall measure of fluid and visuospatial abilities) of 129 and an average *Verbal IQ* (i.e., an overall measure of crystallized ability) of 109.[11] Thus, while still showing a relatively high level of overall intelligence, expert chess players show much better-developed fluid abilities. Steve also shows highly developed spatial abilities, demonstrated by, among other things, his ability to aim his shield and maneuver it through complex geometric patterns, something that has been shown to be highly difficult for others.[12]

Thus far, master chess players, with their highly developed fluid intelligence, still do not seem to have much of an advantage against someone like Tony. There are other, more specific abilities that contribute to chess expertise, though. One notable area in which chess players appear to have an advantage is in problem-solving. More specifically, they seem to excel at planning ahead. Chess players show better performance than non–chess players on tasks requiring planning, a difference that seems to exist independent of IQ.[13] Even when they have no advantage in general intellectual ability, chess players still do better at planning than nonplayers do. Tony is sometimes described as a futurist,[14] someone who predicts future trends, but perhaps this is an area where chess master Steve actually has an advantage.

Another area in which chess players may have a possible advantage is *processing speed*, the ability to perform tasks efficiently, which allows one to perform relatively easy tasks automatically—although the findings are mixed. On one hand, the studies that found them to be better than others at tasks involving planning also found the improved planning ability to be associated with substantially longer time spent making decisions.[15] This suggests that chess players' success at some tasks may be due, not to thinking through possible solutions faster, but simply to taking longer to make decisions. This may suggest they are less impulsive. On the other hand, other studies have found that what differentiates chess players of different skill levels is their ability to perform fast mental processes. Higher ranked chess players perform better not only generally, but also in matches limited to less than 5% of the normal time. In fact, performance in these faster matches accounts for over 80% of the difference between those of high and low skill.[16] This indicates that those more skilled at chess may be better at faster mental processes like recognizing familiar patterns. While it is not entirely clear that chess players have better processing speed, there is at least some evidence, and this would certainly give them an edge over those without the same skill set.

The Downside of Genius

> *"I'm the most intelligent, capable person on the planet. I'm not playing God. All this time, I've been playing human."*
> —Tony Stark, magically disinhibited[17]

A master strategist like Steve clearly has certain advantages. Whether these advantages are sufficient to give him a realistic chance against someone like Tony, however, is another matter entirely. One option available to him is to attempt to exploit Tony's weaknesses. Given his expert chess player's improved recognition ability and long-term planning ability, he has a realistic chance of recognizing these weaknesses.

Tony seems to possess a very high IQ without any significant intellectual limitations. While there do not appear to be any substantial intellectual weaknesses, those with high IQs can still have other limitations. A matter of considerable debate has been whether Attention-Deficit/Hyperactivity Disorder (ADHD) is even a valid diagnosis for individuals with superior intellectual ability.[18] ADHD is a condition marked by an inability to focus or maintain attention, which causes difficulties in functioning. The controversy exists in large part due to the possibility that individuals with high IQ appear inattentive because they find little to challenge them and therefore become bored. In general, however, studies have found that high IQ individuals with ADHD symptoms have severe difficulties in too many areas of life for boredom to explain all symptoms.[19] The fact that intellectually superior individuals can have ADHD does not mean that they do or even that most would be expected to. Likewise, this is not to imply that Tony has ADHD; he is too functional in too many areas. According to the *Diagnostic and Statistical Manual of Mental Disorders – Fifth Edition (DSM-5)*, ADHD can only be diagnosed when someone shows impairment in some major area of life. Tony is highly successful in science, business, and superheroics. While he does sometimes have difficulty getting along with others, this often seems to have more to do with his smug disposition or, at one point, his alcoholism, than to inattention. He does, however, demonstrate some proneness to boredom, which can lead to a degree of inattention. He is constantly moving on to new projects when what he is currently doing can no longer keep his interest. While not ADHD, per se, his tendency to let his focus slip is still a weakness that could be exploited by his enemies.

High IQ can also be associated with traits that can be either advantages or disadvantages. One notable example is *latent inhibition*, the ability to screen out extraneous information, or to decide on an unconscious level not to pay attention to irrelevant stimuli.[20] Traditionally, low levels of this trait have been associated with increased likelihood of psychosis and other mental disorders. Low levels of latent inhibition are also associated with high intellectual ability and creativity, likely because those with low latent inhibition notice things that others don't, resulting in original thinking. Tony's various accomplishments indicate that he is a creative thinker. In addition to understanding a variety of scientific principles, he applies these principles in innovative ways, developing technologies unlike anyone else ever has. For Tony, this trait has clearly been an advantage, but it could be a liability in a combat situation, where one would need to focus on only the most important information,

AUGMENTED INTELLIGENCE

BY JOSUÉ CARDONA

Some researchers state that we are smarter than ever because of technology while others argue that reliance on technology makes humans less intelligent.[21] As Iron Man, Tony Stark has *augmented intelligence*—his own genius enhanced by an artificial intelligence (A.I.) in the form of J.A.R.V.I.S. or later F.R.I.D.A.Y. A person's A.I. assistants can serve to augment cognitive abilities, effectively multiplying that individual's available intelligence.[22] Tony uses A.I. like individuals commonly use technology—to extend cognitive abilities or offset cognitive tasks, such as using a calculator to solve an equation or letting a GPS application decide how to reach a destination.

suggesting another possible liability. That said, latent inhibition has been found to be largely irrelevant to chess performance. Expert chess players appear to be able to process information efficiently and quickly regardless of how well they can inhibit irrelevant information.[23]

The Final Battle

Ultimately, the question is whether a person such as Captain America could realistically have sufficient strategic ability that he could have a chance at defeating a genius like Tony Stark. Steve is a master strategist. In terms of the way he thinks, he has much in common with a master chess player, and mastery of chess has been shown to be independent of overall intellectual ability, which means that someone can excel at strategic thinking even if they are not, strictly speaking, a "genius."[24] Therefore, it is not unrealistic to determine that a better strategist like Steve may be able to better strategize against a genius such as Tony, even lacking Tony's phenomenal intellect. It is also worth noting that, at least in the comic book storyline, Steve does manage to win. He does ultimately surrender, because he believes it to be the right thing to do, but only after his side has already achieved victory.[25]

Comic Book References

Avengers #20 (2013). "The Offer." Script: J. Hickman. Art: L. F. Yu.
Civil War #7 (2007). Script: M. Millar. Art: S. McNiven, D. Vines, J. Dell, & T. Townsend.
Fallen Son: The Death of Captain America #3 (2007). "Bargaining." Script: J. Loeb. Art: J. Romita, Jr. & K. Janson.
Infinity #4 (2013). "Thane." Script: J. Hickman. Art: J. Opeña & D. Weaver.
Iron Man #73–78 (2003–2004,). "The Best Defense." Script: J. J. Miller. Art: J. Lucas.
JLA/Avengers #4 (2003). "The Brave and the Bold." Script: Kurt Busiek. Art: George Perez.
She-Hulk #18 (2007). "Planet Without a Hulk, Part Four: Illuminated." Script: D. Slott. Art: R. Burchett & C. Rathburn.

Superior Iron Man #3 (2015). "Be Superior—Chapter 3: Man of Vision." Script: T. Taylor. Art: Y. Çınar. R. Jose, & J Velasco.

Other References

Anastasi, A., & Urbina, S. (1997). *Psychological testing* (7th ed.). Upper Saddle River, NJ: Prentice Hall.

Antshel, K. M. (2008). Attention-Deficit Hyperactivity Disorder in the context of a high intellectual quotient/giftedness. *Developmental Disabilities Research Reviews*, *14*(4), 293–299.

Burns, B. D. (2004). The effects of speed on skilled chess performance. *Psychological Science*, *15*(7), 442–447.

Carson, S. H., Peterson, J. B., & Higgins, D. M. (2003). Decreased latent inhibition is associated with increased creative achievement in high-functioning individuals. *Journal of Personality and Social Psychology*, *85*(3), 499–506.

Frydman, M., & Lynn, R. (1992). The general intelligence and spatial abilities of gifted young Belgian chess players. *British Journal of Psychology*, *83*(2), 833–835.

Kasparov, G. (2010, February 11). The chess master and the computer. The *New York Times* Review of Books: http://www.nybooks.com/articles/2010/02/11/the-chess-master-and-the-computer/.

Lynn, R. (1992). Does Spearman's *g* decline at high IQ levels? Some evidence from Scotland. *Journal of Genetic Psychology*, *153*(2), 229–230.

Nickerson, R. S. (2005). Technology and cognition amplification. In R. J. Sternberg & D. D. Preiss (Eds.) *Intelligence and technology: The impact of tools on the nature and development of human abilities* (pp. 3–27). Mahwah, NJ: Lawrence Erlbaum.

Postal, V. (2012). Inhibition of irrelevant information is not necessary to performance of expert chess players. *Perceptual & Motor Skills: Learning & Memory*, *115*(1), 60–68.

Salomon, G., & Perkins, D. (2005). Do technologies make us smarter? Intellectual amplification with, of, and through technology. In R. J. Sternberg & D. D. Preiss (Eds.), *Intelligence and technology: The impact of tools on the nature and development of human abilities* (pp. 71–86). Mahwah, NJ: Lawrence Erlbaum.

Schiff, M. M., Kaufman, A. S., & Kaufman, N. L. (1981). Scatter analysis of WISC-R profiles for learning disabled children with superior intelligence. *Journal of Learning Disabilities*, *14*(7), 400–404.

Schinka, J. A., & Vanderploeg, R. D. (2000). Estimating premorbid level of functioning. In Vanderploeg, R. D. (Ed.), *Clinician's guide to neuropsychological assessment, second edition* (pp. 39–67). Mahwah, NJ: Lawrence Erlbaum.

Unterrainer, J. M., Kaller, C. P., Halsband, U., & Rahm, B. (2006). Planning abilities and chess: A comparison of chess and non-chess players on the Tower of London task. *British Journal of Psychology*, *97*(3), 299–311.

Notes

1. *The Avengers* (2012 motion picture).
2. Kasparov (2010).
3. Anastasi & Urbina (1997).
4. Anastasi & Urbina (1997); Schinka & Vanderploeg (2000).
5. Anastasi & Urbina (1997).
6. Schinka & Vanderploeg (2000).

7. Lynn (1992).
8. Schiff et al. (1981).
9. *Iron Man* #73–78 (2003–2004).
10. *Avengers* #20 (2013).
11. Frydman & Lynn (1992).
12. *Fallen Son: The Death of Captain America* #3 (2007).
13. Unterrainer et al. (2006).
14. e.g., *She-Hulk* #18 (2007).
15. Unterrainer et al. (2006).
16. Burns (2004).
17. *Superior Iron Man* #3 (2015).
18. *Antshel* (2008).
19. *Antshel* (2008).
20. Carson et al. (2003).
21. Salomon & Perkins (2005).
22. Nickerson (2005).
23. Postal (2012).
24. Unterrainer et al.(2006).
25. *Civil War* #7 (2007).

EGO

TRAVIS LANGLEY

In Freudian terms, everyone has an ego. It is not an inflated sense of self. In a way, it *is* the self, the mostly conscious part of personality that we think of as ourselves. A battle of wills is a battle of egos, but not necessarily in an egotistical sense. A Freudian view might suggest that we can find the roots of Marvel's superhero conflict in the way young Tony Stark and Steve Rogers experience toilet training, because that's supposedly the way the ego begins to develop. On planet Freud, war may begin in the little boys' room.

Individuals develop much of their self-control during the second and third years of life. Freud said that toilet training teaches patience and self-control and therefore referred to his proposed second psychosexual stage as the *anal stage*. Okay, toilet training plays a part in fostering self-control, true,[1] but that's *not* all there is to it. Erik Erikson, in emphasizing social rather than biological factors, viewed the second psychosocial stage as a crisis of *autonomy vs. shame and doubt*.[2] Erikson would likely view both Captain America and Iron Man more favorably than Freud might because both are *autonomous* (self-sufficient) individuals who are comfortable doing things on their own. Even though Cap often works with partners such as Bucky and the Falcon, his actions suggest that he does not feel inadequate or incomplete without them, does not feel shame for acting independently, and does not dwell on self-doubt. He wants superheroes to enjoy a degree of autonomy that makes Iron Man wary.

People need reasons to wait: benefits for developing self-control and increasing self-sufficiency. A child supposedly learns the *reality principle*, grasping the concept that *delay of gratification* often produces greater satisfaction overall.[3] Freud says that this makes a child more conscious of the external world. With the expansion of the conscious mind, according to psychoanalysts like Freud and Erikson, the mind begins to grow its ego. Steve Rogers and Tony Stark both show a strong grasp of external reality, although in different ways. Socially, for example, Steve is better at seeing people's inner qualities whereas Tony pays more attention to their outward behavior.

Captain America maintains a great degree of self-control. People with strong self-control tend to expect that others will show self-control as well.[4] Such an expectation can become a *self-fulfilling prophecy*[5] when it inspires people to show the expected behavior, and that process in turn provides *behavioral confirmation* of the original expectations.[6] Trusting that other individuals can behave responsibly and stay in control of themselves, Steve believes that individuals can and should take responsibility for themselves without answering to the government.

Iron Man more often struggles to maintain self-control, sometimes losing it through drinking and other hedonistic pleasures. Not trusting that other individuals can behave responsibly and stay in control, maybe as a result of weaknesses in himself, Tony believes that superhuman individuals should let the government force control on them. A Freudian would call this *projection*: He is perceiving his own worst qualities in others because he doesn't have to judge himself as harshly if his weaknesses are common while his strengths remain special.

Projection is one of the *ego defense mechanisms*: things we unknowingly do to protect the ego from anxiety.[7] Even many of the professionals who reject most of Freud's theory speak more favorably of him for initially describing the defense mechanisms and they recognize his daughter Anna Freud for naming most of them and adding to our understanding. We all play tricks on ourselves sometimes.

Instead of coping in healthier ways, numerous ego defense mechanisms involve immature or otherwise unhealthy behavior in people who attempt to avoid stress without facing and solving their problems.[8]

- Tony Stark may be right when he keeps saying he does not have *posttraumatic stress disorder*[9] (a prolonged pattern of avoidance, mood alterations, and related symptoms that result from experiencing trauma[10]), but then again, he may be in *denial* (pathologically denying the reality of a fact that would bother that individual) if acknowledging possible PTSD feels threatening to his self-concept.[11]
- During a period of prolonged stress, he numbs himself through *regression* (immaturely reverting to behavior from an earlier point in life). By resuming his heavy drinking, he falls back into a destructive old habit,[12] and by giving up being Iron Man during that time, he relinquishes what has become his adult place in life.[13]
- Alienating key people in his life, driving them away in a form of social *withdrawal* (very different from substance withdrawal), helps Tony avoid facing what he is doing to himself during his drinking binges.[14] That means growing distant, pulling away, and removing oneself from others.

Defense mechanisms can also be beneficial and healthy. Mature defenses help the ego manage stress and anxiety by solving problems or finding constructive alternatives. These tend to be practical coping behaviors.[15]

- In place of acting on an impulse that the ego finds unacceptable, anything a person does as a distraction is a form of *sublimation* (taking the impulse to do one thing and channeling it into another activity). Shortly after Tony first quits drinking,[16] he throws himself into designing and building a wider variety of specialized armor.[17] Steve sometimes relies on his art to relieve stress.[18]
- Both become heroes at least partly out of *compensation*, making up for their weaknesses by building other strengths in helpful ways.
- They also inspire others who emulate in a form of *identification* with them, feeling more complete as people by incorporating another person's qualities into themselves—ranging from children who dress in costumes to other superheroes who adopt symbols, colors, or whole outfits modeled after theirs.

Developing a secure ego with healthy self-control might make it easier for a person later to abide by personal priorities, ethics, standards, and a sense of morality.[19] Even though Freud's ideas on the reasons (sex[20]) why our cognitive and moral awareness progresses in the order that it does may be mere speculation,[21] other professionals also have observed, both anecdotally and through methodical research, that the roots of our self-control grow before our awareness of essential morality begins to blossom, all around the same ages that Freud observed.[22] Self-control makes it easier for people to be heroic—to overcome the odds, fight for a cause, adhere to ideals, and listen to that thing Freud called the *superego*, the conscience (which we'll take a look at in Depth File III: Superego).

Comic Book References

Captain America #237 (1979). "From the Ashes . . ." Script/story: C. Claremont & R. McKenzie. Art: S. Buscema & D. Perlin.

Iron Man #127 (1979). "A Man's Home Is His Battlefield. . . ." Script: D. Michelinie. Art: J. Romita Jr. & B. Layton.

Iron Man #128 (1979). "Demon in a Bottle." Script/story: D. Michelinie & B. Layton. Art: J. Romita Jr. & B. Layton.

Iron Man #142 (1981). "Sky-Die." Script/story: D. Micheline & B. Layton. Art: J. Romita Jr. & B. Layton.

Iron Man #152 (1981). "Escape from Heaven's Hand!" Script/story: D. Micheline & B. Layton. Art: J. Romita Jr. & B. Layton.

Iron Man #167 (1983). "The Empty Shell." Writer: D. O'Neil. Art: L. McDonnell & S. Mitchell.

Iron Man #170 (1983). "And Who Shall Clothe Himself in Iron?" Script: D. O'Neil. Art: L. McDonnell & S. Mitchell.

Other References

American Psychiatric Association (2013). *Diagnostic and statistical manual of mental disorders* (DSM-5). Washington, DC: American Psychiatric Association.

Antonaccio, O. & Tittle, C. R. (2008). Morality, self-control, and crime. *Criminology: An Interdisciplinary Journal, 46*(2), 479–510.

Baumeister, R. F. (2000). Self-control, morality, and human strength. *Journal of Social and Clinical Psychology, 19*(1), 29–42.

Bell, D. B., Dolin, S. F., Houston, T. J., & Krisiansen, D. M. (1973). Predictions and self-fulfilling prophecies of army discipline. *Proceedings of the Annual Convention of the American Psychological Association 1973*, 747–748.

Cavell, M. (2001). Seeing through Freud. *Annual of Psychoanalysis, 29*, 67–82.

Cox, D. J., Morris, J. B., Borowitz, S. M., & Sutphen, J. L. (2002). Psychological differences between children with and without chronic encopresis. *Journal of Pediatric Psychology, 27*(7), 585–591.

Diamond, S. (2010, March 10). *Normalcy, neurosis, and psychosis: What is a mental disorder? Psychology Today:* http://www.psychologytoday.com/blog/evil-deeds/201003/normalcy-neurosis-and-psychosis-what-is-mental-disorder.

Erikson, E. (1950). *Childhood and society.* New York, NY: Norton.

Freud, A. (1936). *The ego and the mechanisms of defense.* London, UK: Hogarth.

Freud, S. (1911). Formulations regarding the two principles in mental functioning. In *Collected papers* (vol. 4, pp. 13–21). London, UK: Hogarth.

Freud, S. (1940). An outline of psychoanalysis. In *Standard edition of the complete works of Sigmund Freud* (vol. 23, pp. 141–207). London, UK: Hogarth.

Kohlberg, L. (1973). *Essays on moral development.* San Francisco, CA: Harper & Row.

Koriat, A., & Nisan, M. (1977). The nature of conflict in delay of gratification. *Journal of Genetic Psychology: Research and Theory on Human Development, 131*(2), 195–205.

Koval, C. Z., van Dellen, M. R., Fitzsimons, G. M., & Ranby, K. W. (2015). The burden of responsibility: Interpersonal costs of high self-control. *Journal of Personality and Social Psychology, 108*(5), 750–766.

Langley, T. (2013a, May 4). *Does Iron Man 3's hero suffer posttraumatic stress disorder?* Psychology Today: https://www.psychologytoday.com/blog/beyond-heroes-and-villains/201305/does-iron-man-3s-hero-suffer-posttraumatic-stress-disorder.

Langley, T. (2013b, May 5). *Twitter takes on Iron Man 3: Why can't Tony Stark sleep?* Psychology Today: https://www.psychologytoday.com/blog/beyond-heroes-and-villains/201305/twitter-takes-iron-man-3-why-cant-tony-stark-sleep.

Langley, T. (2015). Eros, thanatos, and an armory of defense mechanisms: Sigmund Freud in the land of the dead. In T. Langley (Ed.), *The Walking Dead psychology: Psych of the living dead* (pp. 192–205). New York, NY: Sterling.

Letamendi, A. (2013, May 10). *Iron Man: A terrible privilege.* Under the Mask: http://www.underthemaskonline.com/iron-man-a-terrible-privilege/.

Metzger, J. A. (2014). Adaptive defense mechanisms: Function and transference. *Journal of Clinical Psychology, 7*(5), 478–488.

Musser, L. M., & Graziano, W. G. (1991). Behavioral confirmation in children's interactions with peers. *Basic and Applied Social Psychology, 12*(4), 441–456.

Piaget, J. (1932). *The moral judgment of the child.* New York, NY: Harcourt Brace.

Rosenthal, R., & Jacobsen, L. (1968). *Pygmalion in the classroom.* New York, NY: Holt, Rinehart & Winston.

Snyder, M., & Klein, O. (2005). Construing and constructing others: On the reality and the generality of the behavior confirmation scenario. *Social Behaviour and Communication in Biological and Artificial Systems, 6*(1), 53–67.

Vaillant, G. E. (1977). *Adaptation to life.* Boston, MA: Little, Brown.

Notes

1. Cox et al. (2002).
2. Erikson (1950).
3. Freud (1911); Koriat & Nisan (1977).
4. Koval et al. (2015).
5. Bell et al. (1973); Rosenthal & Jacobsen (1968).
6. Musser & Graziano (1991); Snyder & Klein (2005).
7. Freud (1936).
8. Diamond (2010); Langley (2015); Vaillant (1977).
9. *Iron Man 3* (2013 motion picture).
10. American Psychiatric Association (2013).
11. Langley (2013a, 2013b); Letamendi (2013).
12. *Iron Man* #167 (1983).
13. *Iron Man* #170 (1983).
14. *Iron Man* #127 (1979).
15. Metzger (2014); Vaillant (1977).
16. *Iron Man* #128 (1979).
17. *Iron Man* #142, 152 (1981); *Iron Man 3* (2013 motion picture).
18. *Captain America* #237 (1979); *Captain America: The First Avenger* (2011 motion picture).
19. Antonaccio & Tittle (2008); Baumeister (2000).
20. Freud (1940).
21. Cavell (2001).
22. Kohlberg (1973); Piaget (1932).

PART THREE

IDEALS

When heroes clash with other heroes, their issues might not be as simple a matter as discerning dark from light. When they're all right from their own points of view, the time comes to revisit the ways we all make moral decisions and perhaps redefine what we'll call "moral" at all.

CHAPTER EIGHT

WILD HEROES: THE HARD WORK OF BEING "MORAL"

ERIC D. WESSELMANN AND J. SCOTT JORDAN

"The same behavior can be interpreted as good or evil depending on which side of the fence the perceiver happens to be on . . ."
—psychologist Linda J. Skitka[1]

"Civil War is about what happens when the Marvel heroes are forced to grow up. It's as simple as that."
—comic book writer Mark Millar[2]

People learn concepts of morality from their cultural myths, rituals, and institutions.[3] Once people have adopted a moral framework, they tend to assume moral decisions are simple: There are things that are "right" and things that are "wrong." While people may differ on the specific contents of these beliefs, a commonality is that they endorse these beliefs intuitively.[4] For example, this tendency is illustrated in *Civil War* when a majority of the superheroes initially pick a specific side and believe it to be morally correct. As *Civil War* continues however, the ensuing conflicts cause many of the characters to question their moral beliefs. This arc from moral *certainty* to moral *ambiguity* lies at the heart of both *Civil War* and the psychology of morality.

The Journey to Become "Moral"

Psychologists have studied moral development and decision-making since the field's inception.[5] The most impactful older theories viewed moral thinking as a specific outcome of cognitive development: As people age they become capable of increasingly sophisticated reasoning and conceptualization of abstract ideals.[6] Lawrence Kohlberg, the most iconic theorist from this perspective, argued people may progress through upwards of six developmental stages, each one focused on more abstract ideas about justice.[7] These stages are commonly discussed in the context of three broader levels: preconventional, conventional, and postconventional levels.[8]

Preconventional Morality

In *preconventional* moral reasoning, people judge morality predominately on the self-focused benefits (or punishments) that result from their behavior. Members of the Thunderbolts, a group of government-employed supervillains, are ordered to hunt down Spider-Man after he defects from Iron Man's side to Captain America's. They only refrain from killing Spider-Man because Iron Man and S.H.I.E.L.D. have implanted microscopic nanobots in each member that will electrocute them if they disobey orders.[9] As such, these supervillains' morality would be categorized in the lowest level of development because they obey authority simply to avoid punishment.

Conventional Morality

In the *conventional* level, people judge morality predominately on whether or not the action maintains or disrupts social order (defined by laws or sociocultural norms). Iron Man, his allies, and many regular citizens criticize Captain America and his followers for breaking the law as dictated by the U.S. government and its citizens.[10] For these people, the choice of whether an act is right or wrong depends solely on whether or not the act conforms to the letter of the law.

Postconventional Morality

Finally, in the *postconventional* level, people judge morality predominately on whether or not an action violates a personal or universal code of ethics that may supersede institutional authority, laws, or cultural norms. Captain America's credo throughout *Civil War* is that the Superhero Registration Act, even if it may be an official *law*, is a violation of the basic *principles* on which the United States was founded.[11] Captain America's moral decisions hinge upon whether or not the abstract ideals he holds sacred are being preserved by his actions.

The "Rightness" of Kohlberg's Moral Theory

At first glance, Kohlberg's theory of morality may seem simple; all you have to do is develop the right level of cognitive reasoning and you will develop the "right" morality. However, Kohlberg notes that a person's moral development is not a linear trajectory that naturally progresses with each passing year. People's moral growth may become stunted if they do not also receive adequate socialization from parents, teachers, and friends.[12] Indeed, some people may reach adult-hood without ever progressing beyond an immature form of moral thought. Further, the culture one is raised in may produce different beliefs about what the "right" thing to do is, regardless of one's cognitive abilities. In *Civil War*, many characters change their moral views because of particular events and not because they reach a new level of developmentally based cognitive reasoning. For example, when Iron Man confesses to the seemingly dead body of Captain America that the conflict "wasn't worth it,"[13] it is not because he has suddenly developed the capacity for more abstract ways of thinking. Rather, he makes this confession because he realizes his actions have brought about the death of a beloved friend. Throughout *Civil War*, most of the moral questioning the characters engage in emerges from the specific conflicts they are experiencing, not because they are making transitions between cognitive stages.

The Struggle to Stay "Moral"

Because most of us live complicated lives and often have to say or do things that conflict with our cultural norms, rules, or ideals, many psychologists investigate how we deal with these moral conflicts. When such a conflict occurs, people experience a type of cognitive dissonance termed *moral/ethical dissonance*.[14] Generally, dissonance is unpleasant and this discomfort is intensified when it involves morals that are core aspects of people's identity; thus, people reduce the dissonance any way they can.[15] If the situation around the moral conflict is sufficiently ambiguous, people may cognitively reinterpret their immoral behavior to convince themselves (and others) that the behavior was well-intentioned or done for altruistic reasons (e.g., "for the

greater good").[16] Iron Man demonstrates this type of reinter-
pretation when he uses his technology to spy on Spider-Man
while they are working together[17] and when he works with
S.H.I.E.L.D. to employ supervillains.[18] Captain America also
reinterprets his own behavior as the war intensifies, for example, when he works with the Punisher[19] and when he uses a
secret weapon against Iron Man under the guise of a parley.[20]

Another strategy people use to remove moral/ethical dissonance is to compare their own questionable conflicted behavior with conflicted behaviors performed by others (especially
members of rival out-groups) to convince themselves that their
behaviors are less immoral than others' behaviors.[21] Both Iron
Man and Captain America argue during a secret meeting about
who crossed the moral boundaries first and who has sunk the
lowest, and it eventually devolves into a fistfight.[22]

As another example of reducing dissonance, if peoples'
immoral behaviors are not ambiguous enough to be cognitively reframed, they may resort to compensation through
restitution or future moral behaviors designed to communicate
moral conversion.[23] Iron Man confesses to Captain America
that one reason he supports the Superhero Registration Act is
because he nearly killed innocent bystanders during a drunken
rage, so he could have just as easily been responsible for a tragedy like the Stamford Incident.[24] Indeed, it seems like Iron
Man is trying just as hard to expiate his personal guilt as he is
the guilt for the superhero community broadly.[25]

People also reduce moral/ethical dissonance by adjust-
ing their degree of commitment to moral convictions. Once
people form moral systems, these systems become worldviews
that motivate how people perceive the motives and actions
of others, and ultimately their attitudes and voting behavior on various sociopolitical issues.[26] People often experience
these attitudes on moral issues as *convictions*—self-evident facts

that need no justification or debate.[27] For example, Captain America defends his opposition to the Superhero Registration Act by arguing that the act is "wrong, plain and simple,"[28] and that "what's right is right."[29] When a person perceives one of their convictions to be threatened, it can cause them to endorse their views more extremely.[30] Throughout *Civil War*, with each conflict, Captain American and Iron Man become increasingly entrenched in their positions and are willing to take greater risks to defend their views.[31]

Moral convictions also provide individuals the courage to continue a course of action, even if it means that person will face ridicule, discrimination, or other great personal costs.[32] When Captain America surrenders, he adjusts his moral conviction that it was "right" to resist the Superhero Registration Act and, instead, comes to believe that, although his side may have been technically winning the battle, they were losing the argument because their actions were violating the ideals they were defending.[33] His new moral conviction, that his resistance was no longer the "right" thing to do, provides him the courage he needs to surrender, knowing it would likely mean he would be tried and executed for treason.[34] Even the Punisher, a homicidal vigilante, has lines that he will not cross: Captain America beats him up for killing supervillains but the Punisher refuses to fight back because of what Captain America symbolizes to him.[35] An unintended consequence of increasing one's moral conviction is that it affords people the opportunity to engage in horrible acts if they believe they have the moral high ground.[36] Both Captain America and Iron Man engage in morally questionable behavior because they believe they are on the "right side," and as the war continues, they become increasingly entrenched in their perspectives, regardless of the collateral damage incurred by their conflict.

Redefining "Moral"

Because being moral requires people to continuously manage various conflicts across and within different levels of self-identity, many contemporary psychological theories have abandoned the idea that morality is about simply doing the "right" thing. Instead, they propose that morality is a contextual, agreed-upon standard driven largely by culture[37] that forces individuals to continuously negotiate moral conflicts at various levels of identity.[38]

Haidt[39] states that cultures differ on the aspects of what they consider to be morally "right" or "wrong" predominately on what helps the group bond and sustain itself successfully.[40] The values that best fulfill these functions for a group often become imbued with a type of "sacredness," regardless of whether they have any direct religious or spiritual connotations.[41]

There are five basic themes that form the basis of most moral systems found cross-culturally: harm/care, fairness/reciprocity, in-group/loyalty, authority/respect, and purity/sanctity. Specific cultures and their members may vary on how much value they place in each theme, but all themes are present to some degree.[42] However, how people specifically define the application of each of these themes can differ, even within cultures[43]; we see examples of each theme and the nuances of their application on both sides in *Civil War*.

Harm/Care

Morality based on *harm/care* focuses on minimizing the pain or suffering others experience and avoiding any behaviors that would cause harm to others. Iron Man makes it a priority to instruct his allies to avoid harming any innocent bystanders while fighting crime.[44] Captain America surrenders when he finally becomes aware of the destruction they are causing and the threat their conflict poses to average citizens.[45]

Fairness/Reciprocity

Morality based on *fairness/reciprocity* focuses on protecting equality and justice for all people. Iron Man argues that superheroes should be held to the same accountability, ethical standards, and federal oversight as police, firefighters, and soldiers.[46] Captain America focuses on fairness as an issue of personal freedom and views the Superhero Registration Act as wrong precisely because it takes away the superheroes freedoms and autonomy.[47]

In-group/Loyalty

Morality based on *in-group/loyalty* focuses on strengthening individual attachments to established social groups (e.g., family, country) and safeguarding those groups' unity and well-being. Iron Man cares about both the nation and superhero community and states that he wants to spearhead the pro-registration movement as a way to make sure that the federal government does not exploit superheroes.[48] Captain America cares about both these groups as well, but Iron Man points out to him that his versions of these two groups are idealized and not necessarily relevant to modern times.[49]

Authority/Respect

Morality based on *authority/respect* focuses on respect for social hierarchies and obedience to established authority. A person following such concepts puts the government's opinion and belief above all other opinions and goals. For example, Iron Man and his allies demonstrate respect for authority as mandated by federal law (i.e., the Superhero Registration Act) while Captain America respects the authority of the U.S. Constitution and not necessarily the elected officials who are supposed to be upholding it.[50]

Purity/Sanctity

Morality based on *purity/sanctity* focuses on avoiding contamination or corruption, whether at a biological or spiritual/ethical level. Recovering alcoholics like Iron Man view returning to drinking as a dire moral threat that would contaminate their judgment and self-concept—Iron Man struggles with such fears. He takes solace in the fact that at the end of the conflict he still had remained sober.[51] Others without such direct and personal self-fears—heroes like Captain America—view maintaining their principles as the true struggle in the conflict and make decisions guided and controlled by their moral compass. Changing purpose and fundamental beliefs are impossible—learning from mistakes is not a purported goal or material focus—Captain America is an example as he argues that Iron Man was the real loser because he compromised his principles from the outset.[52]

Whose Side Should We Pick?

The arc from moral certainty to moral ambiguity is reflected in not only the individual characters of *Civil War*, but the writing style as well. At the outset, the reader is encouraged to adopt a hard-line point of view. The promotional campaign asked, "Whose Side Are You On?"[53] and Marvel provided stickers at conventions proudly proclaiming "I'm with Captain America" or "I'm with Iron Man." However, as the arc of *Civil War* plays out, the writers never let one view become the "right" view. Rather, it's as if the authors have taken the position of Dr. Strange, when he says, "There is no right or wrong in this debate. It is simply a matter of perspective, and it is not my place to influence the evolution of the superhuman role."[54]

This certainty-ambiguity arc has also occurred in the field of psychology. Decades ago, psychologists treated morality as a developmentally based cognitive, decision-making process.[55] Psychologists believed that as people developed the capacity for more sophisticated thinking, their moral decisions likewise became more sophisticated and transitioned from being primarily *self*-centered to more *other*-focused. This *other*-focused way of thinking was treated as the "right" and moral way to think and behave. Contemporary theories tend to conceptualize morality in terms of each individual's unique struggle to manage their ongoing relationships with family, friends, institutions, and culture.[56] From this perspective, there is no "right" way for every person to be. Rather, morality is defined as contextually dependent social management, and it is more about "lived life" than "abstract principles." Said another way, morality is wild— being moral is about the daily work of negotiating and managing our relationships with others.[57]

Comic Book References

Amazing Spider-Man #534 (2006). "The War at Home," part 3. Script: M. Straczynski. Art: R. Garney & B. Reinhold.

Amazing Spider-Man #536 (2006). "The War at Home," part 5. Script: M. Straczynski. Art: R. Garney & B. Reinhold.

Captain America #22 (2006). "The Drums of War," part 1. Script: E. Brubaker. Art: M. Perkins.

Civil War #1–7 (2006–2007). Script: M. Millar. Art: S. McNiven, D. Vines, & M. Morales.

Civil War: Frontline #7 (2006). "Embedded," part 7. Script: P. Jenkins. Art: R. Bachs & J. Lucas.

Civil War: Frontline #9 (2007). "Embedded," part 9. Script: P. Jenkins. Art: R. Bachs & J. Lucas.

Civil War: Frontline #10 (2007). "The Accused," part 10. Script: P. Jenkins. Art: S. Lieber.

Civil War: Frontline #11 (2007). "Embedded," part 11. Script: P. Jenkins. Art: R. Bachs & J. Lucas.

Civil War: Opening Shot (2006). Script: J. McCann. Art: Various.

Civil War: The Confession (2007). Script: B. M. Bendis. Art: A. Maleev.

Iron Man #13 (2006). Script: D. Knauf & C. Knauf. Art: Art: P. Zircher & S. Hanna.

Iron Man #14 (2006). Script: D. Knauf & C. Knauf. Art: P. Zircher & S. Hanna.

Iron Man/Captain America: Casualties of War #1 (2007). Script: C. N. Gage. Art: J. Haun & M. Morales.

Marvel Spotlight: Mark Millar/Steve McNiven (2006). Writer/coordinator: J. R. Thomas. Artist: None.

New Avengers: Illuminati (2006). Script: B. M. Bendis. Art: A. Maleev.

References

Ayal, S., & Gino, F. (2012). Honest rationales for dishonest behavior. In M. Mikulincer & P. R. Shaver (Eds.), *The social psychology of morality: Exploring the causes of good and evil* (pp. 149–166). Washington, DC: American Psychological Association.

Bastian, B., Jetten, J., & Fasoli, F. (2011). Cleansing the soul by hurting the flesh: The guilt-reducing effect of pain. *Psychological Science, 22*(3), 334–335.

Campbell, J., & Moyers, B. (2011). *The power of myth*. New York, NY: Anchor Books.

Festinger, L. (1962). Cognitive dissonance. *Scientific American, 207*(4), 93–102.

Frimer, J. A., Tell, C. E., & Haidt, J. (2015). Liberals condemn sacrilege too: The harmless desecration of Cerro Torre. *Social Psychological and Personality Science, 6*(8), 878–886.

Graham, J., & Haidt, J. (2012). Sacred values and evil adversaries: A moral foundations approach. In M. Mikulincer & P. R. Shaver (Eds.), *The social psychology of morality: Exploring the causes of good and evil* (pp. 11–31). Washington, DC: American Psychological Association.

Graham, J., Haidt, J., & Nosek, B. A. (2009). Liberals and conservatives rely on different sets of moral foundations. *Journal of Personality and Social Psychology, 96*(5), 1029–1046.

Greenberg, J., & Jonas, E. (2003). Psychological motives and political orientation—The left, the right, and the rigid: Comment on Jost et al. (2003). *Psychological Bulletin, 129*(3), 376–382.

Haidt, J. (2007). The new synthesis in moral psychology. *Science, 316*(5827), 998–1002.

Haidt, J. (2008). Morality. *Perspectives on Psychological Science, 3*(1), 65–72.

Haidt, J. & Graham, J. (2007). When morality opposes justice: Conservatives have moral intuitions that liberals may not recognize. *Social Justice Research, 20*(1), 98–116.

Haidt, J., Graham, J., & Joseph, C. (2009). Above and below left–right: Ideological narratives and moral foundations. *Psychological Inquiry, 20*(2–3), 110–119.

Janoff-Bulman, R. (2012). Conscience: The dos and don'ts of moral regulation. In M. Mikulincer & P. R. Shaver (Eds.), *The social psychology of morality: Exploring the causes of good and evil* (pp. 131–148). Washington, DC: American Psychological Association.

Jordan, J. S., & Wesselmann, E. D. (2015). The contextually grounded nature of prosocial behavior: A multi-scale, embodied approach to morality. In W. G. Graziano & D. Schroeder (Eds.), *Oxford handbook of prosocial behavior* (pp. 153–165). New York, NY: Oxford University Press.

Jost, J. T., Glaser, J., Kruglanski, A. W., & Sulloway, F. J. (2003). Political conservatism as motivated social cognition. *Psychological Bulletin, 129*(3), 339–375.

Klaassen, J. A. (1996). Punishment and the purification of moral taint. *Journal of Social Philosophy, 27*(2), 51–64.

Kohlberg, L. (1984). *The psychology of moral development: The nature and validity of moral stages*. San Francisco, CA: Harper & Row.

Koleva, S. P., Graham, J., Iyer, R., Ditto, P. H., & Haidt, J. (2012). Tracing the threads: How five moral concerns (especially purity) help explain culture war attitudes. *Journal of Research in Personality, 46*(2), 184–194.

McAdams, D. P., Albaugh, M., Farber, E., Daniels, J., Logan, R. L., & Olson, B. (2008). Family metaphors and moral intuitions: How conservatives and liberals narrate their lives. *Journal of Personality and Social Psychology, 95*(4), 978–990.

Monin, B. & Merritt, A. (2012). Moral hypocrisy, moral inconsistency, and the struggle for moral integrity. In M. Mikulincer & P. R. Shaver (Eds.), *The social psychology of morality: Exploring the causes of good and evil* (pp. 167–184). Washington, DC: American Psychological Association.

Nairne, J. S. (2011). *Psychology* (5th ed.). Belmont, CA: Wadsworth.

Nelissen, R., & Zeelenberg, M. (2009). When guilt evokes self-punishment: Evidence for the existence of a Dobby Effect. *Emotion, 9*(1), 118–122.

Piaget, J. (1932/1965). *The moral judgment of the child.* Glencoe, IL: Free Press.

Segal, R. A. (2004). *Myth: A very short introduction.* New York, NY: Oxford University Press.

Skitka, L. J. (2012). Moral convictions and moral courage: Common denominators of good and evil. In M. Mikulincer & P. R. Shaver (Eds.), *The social psychology of morality: Exploring the causes of good and evil* (pp. 349–365). Washington, DC: American Psychological Association.

Tangney, J. P. (2003). Self-relevant emotions. In M. R. Leary & J. P. Tangney (Eds), *Handbook of self and identity* (pp. 384–400). New York, NY: Guilford.

Wallington, S. A. (1973). Consequences of transgression: Self-punishment and depression. *Journal of Personality and Social Psychology, 28*(1), 1–7.

Notes

1. Skitka (2012), pg. 350.
2. *Marvel Spotlight: Mark Millar/Steve McNiven* (2006).
3. Haidt, (2007; 2008); Campbell & Moyers (2011); Segal (2004).
4. Haidt (2008).
5. Haidt (2008).
6. Kohlberg (1984); Piaget (1932/1965).
7. Kohlberg (1984).
8. Haidt (2008); Nairne (2011).
9. *Civil War* #5 (2006).
10. *Captain America* #22 (2006); *Civil War* #1 (2006); *Civil War* #3 (2006); *Iron Man/Captain America: Casualties of War* #1 (2007).
11. *Captain America* #22 (2006); *Civil War: Frontline* #9 (2007); *Iron Man/Captain America: Casualties of War* #1 (2007).
12. Kohlberg (1984).
13. *Civil War: The Confession* (2007).
14. Ayal & Gino (2012).
15. Festinger (1962).
16. Ayal & Gino (2012); Monin & Merritt (2012).
17. *Amazing Spider-Man* #534 (2006); *Iron Man* #14 (2006).
18. *Civil War* #4 (2006).
19. *Civil War* #5–6.
20. *Civil War* #3 (2006).
21. Ayal & Gino (2012).
22. *Iron Man/Captain America: Casualties of War* #1 (2007).
23. Ayal & Gino (2012); Janoff-Bulman (2012); Monin & Merritt (2012).
24. *Iron Man/Captain America: Casualties of War* #1 (2007).
25. *Iron Man* #13 (2006).
26. Graham et al. (2009); Haidt et al. (2009); Jost et al. (2003); McAdams et al. (2008).
27. Skitka (2012).
28. *Captain America* #22 (2006).
29. *Iron Man/Captain America: Casualties of War* #1 (2007).
30. Greenberg & Jonas (2003).
31. *Civil War* #1–7 (2006–2007).

32. Skitka (2012).
33. *Civil War* #7 (2007).
34. *Civil War: The Confession* (2007).
35. *Civil War* #6 (2007).
36. Graham & Haidt (2012).
37. Haidt (2008).
38. Jordan & Wesselmann (2015).
39. Haidt (2008).
40. Haidt & Graham (2007); Haidt (2008).
41. Graham & Haidt (2012).
42. Haidt et al. (2009).
43. Frimer et al. (2015); Koleva et al. (2012).
44. *Iron Man* #13 (2006).
45. *Civil War* #7 (2007).
46. *Iron Man/Captain America: Casualties of War* #1 (2007).
47. *Iron Man/Captain America: Casualties of War* #1 (2007).
48. *New Avengers: Illuminati* (2006).
49. *Iron Man/Captain America: Casualties of War* #1 (2007).
50. *Civil War: Frontline* #11 (2007).
51. *Civil War: The Confession* (2007).
52. *Civil War: The Confession* (2007).
53. *Civil War: Opening Shot* (2006).
54. *Civil War* #6 (2007).
55. Kohlberg (1984); Piaget (1932/1965).
56. Haidt (2008); Jordan & Wesselmann (2015).
57. Jordan & Wesselmann (2015).

Whether we see them in our lives, on the news, or in entertainment of any kind, role models can influence our behavior through observational learning, but why does this happen? How it is that the actions of role models can influence our own even when we observe them without direct interaction? Could a mask ever help that happen?

CHAPTER NINE

A SHIELD BY ANY OTHER NAME: THE POWER OF THE PROSOCIAL ROLE MODEL IN A MASK

ALEX LANGLEY

"The price of freedom is high, and if I'm the only one
willing to pay it, so be it.
But I'm willing to bet I'm not."
—Captain America[1]

> *"Even the self-assured will raise their perceived self-efficacy*
> *if models teach them better ways of doing things."*
> —psychologist Albert Bandura[2]

Steve Rogers is dead. Captain America lives.
A person is mortal. That person's symbols are not. After someone dies or leaves us in other ways, the things that person represents—everything the individual psychologically

symbolizes for us—can endure.[3] The reverse holds true as well: Symbols of that person persist in the form of photographs, memories, objects, and words,[4] along with actions that others might take in the departed one's honor or name.

There is something about Captain America that inspires others to become better than they think they can be. Although he was originally created as a "patriotically-themed superhero,"[5] Captain America has become more than a mere symbol of American patriotism: He's one of Marvel Comics' most universally known prosocial models.

What makes a role model? Why do some people emulate certain role models more than others? How exactly does a hero who seems larger than life come to inspire people to be better?

Eyes Watching, Minds Learning

Albert Bandura's groundbreaking research on *observational learning*, a type of social learning in which an individual learns behavior patterns by first observing them in others,[6] helps explain the influential power our behaviors hold over those who observe them. In the case of Captain America and Bucky, Cap's example serves as a *prosocial model* to Bucky, bolstering his moral strength and encouraging him to do good deeds as a result of watching Cap do just that. The model demonstrates the behavior from which the observer may learn. In Bandura's Bobo doll experiment, however, we see the influence of observational learning used to foster negative behaviors. Bandura took several groups of children and exposed them to different sets of modeled behaviors. Both groups were exposed to a female model in a room full of toys, with a Bobo doll (an inflatable punching bag with a picture of a clown on it) being the primary focus. In the experimental scenario, the model behaved aggressively toward the Bobo doll, beating it savagely and verbally abusing him. In the control scenario, the model did not engage in those behaviors. The children then were allowed to play in the playroom, and their behaviors were recorded. Bandura found that the children who were exposed to the aggressive model behaved more aggressively toward Bobo, even mimicking unique actions and language specific to the model. Those who were not exposed to the aggressive model were significantly less aggressive. Bandura found that girls were more affected by the aggressive display, supporting his theory about the increased influential power of same-sex modeling. Simply put, kids who saw bad *did* bad. If the children had been presented with a model who behaved kindly toward Bobo, one might expect them to have reacted by treating the doll with kindness as well. If the model had put a domino mask on Bobo and enlisted him as a sidekick in a quest to fight injustice, we probably would have seen a small army of children punching bad guys alongside their sidekick, Bobo.

Although most remember Bandura for his experiment highlighting the ways human beings potentially learn negative behaviors from one another, he also had a more optimistic side. Among other things, he extensively studied *self-efficacy*,[7] our ability to change our situations for the better—an idea Cap both espouses to others and shows through his actions.

Goodness Inspiring Goodness

Observational learning can confer great prosocial benefits in the correct circumstances. Both teenagers and medical students were more likely to think and behave altruistically after being presented with a prosocial model (and if prompted to reflect on the significance of that model).[8] Although it's unlikely that any of us will have to fight off invading aliens or destroy rampaging robots the way Captain America does, there are plenty of positive choices we can make in our lives by reaching out to others with a supportive word or figuring out ways to overcome our self-imposed limits. Captain America often encourages others to engage in prosocial behaviors, whether it's rallying his fellow heroes to defeat the villains, encouraging World War II America to buy war bonds, or trying to get kids to pick up trash in their neighborhoods.[9] This encouragement can have far-reaching real-world impact, especially on those who are willing to engage cognitively with what they have just seen or read.

Prosocial actions and interpersonal skills such as forgiveness and empathy often go hand in hand; individuals with increased altruistic tendencies were more likely to employ forgiveness and empathy in their dealings with others, and those who were taught empathy were more likely to become forgiving and altruistic.[10] Other research on Bandura's theory of observational learning has shown that individuals who do not experience forgiveness from others or see forgiveness between others not only have difficulty expressing it themselves but also have difficulty understanding the emotions of others and are more inclined to make self-centered rather than altruistic decisions.[11] Even after Bucky unwittingly helps destroy S.H.I.E.L.D., Cap forgives him and reaches out to him with compassion. As a result, Bucky chooses to save Cap's life rather than end it. Receiving forgiveness can rekindle innate altruistic tendencies in a person who may have strayed from them.[12] "I'm with you 'til the end of the line,"[13] Rogers assures him. That promise leads to repercussions for the cinematic Avengers,[14] but Cap is consistent and will not break a promise. When a person becomes associated with emotionally laden ideals, symbolic power like Captain America's stays strongest if the way he embodies those concepts remains reliable and true.[15]

When the living legend falls, seemingly assassinated in the comic books,[16] his former sidekick Bucky takes up his shield and his mantle, becoming Captain America[17] as a tribute to both Steve and the legacy of his heroism and as a mechanism to deal with his own *bereavement* (perhaps because altruistic behavior can be a healthy way to cope[18]). That cause? Taking on the mantle of his mentor and becoming a better person thanks to years of learning from his role model (a process known as *social modeling*[19]).

Putting Others First

There is a delicate balance between freedom and security, and whereas his fellow Avenger Iron Man may fall on the side of security, Captain America believes in freedom. In the face of Hydra's seemingly endless infestation of the ranks of S.H.I.E.L.D., Captain America puts his life on the line to protect everyone who would be harmed by the corrupted Project Insight. More specifically, he believes in the basic willingness of others to do the right thing when given the choice rather than passively default to doing nothing (known as the *default effect*[20]), as evidenced by his speech to the hundreds of S.H.I.E.L.D. agents still at their headquarters.[21] With Cap's prosocial example emboldening them, those agents rise up against Hydra despite the potential costs to their lives, choosing the *altruistic* thing to do over the safe thing to do.

The Real Power of Fictional Characters

Merely thinking about familiar prosocial models can instigate positive behaviors. In one study,[22] children age 6 through 12 years were presented with pictures of neutral models and prosocial models that included comic book superheroes, along with paired photos of healthy and unhealthy foods. With each presentation, children indicated which of the foods they thought their heroes would eat. Afterward, when choosing their own foods, the children who believed their heroes would eat healthy were significantly more likely to choose healthy (apple "fries") food over unhealthy (French fries) food. The more the children admired their prosocial models and the more often they selected healthy food as the food of choice for those superheroes, the more likely they were to make a healthy choice for themselves.

Encouraging children to take the perspective of prosocial models such as superheroes helped them achieve greater empathy and cognitive functioning through increased distance from the self, with children roughly five years of age getting the most benefit from this thought exercise.[23] Children who were able to achieve this self-distance not only gained better understanding of the perspectives of others but were inclined toward greater degrees of self-control, as self-distancing gave them better abilities to distance themselves from their current situation and think about the future implications of their current decisions.

Piaget's research on cognitive development in human beings found that during our earliest stages of cognition we engage in *egocentrism*, an inability to take the perspective of others.[24] Although most people acquire some level of perspective taking ability over time, moving away from the purely egocentric view they had as young children, it's a skill that should be encouraged and trained for maximum effectiveness. Doing something as simple as asking children what they believe Captain America would do in a given situation is a good way to help them see things from someone else's point of view, increasing their empathy skills when they are needed in real-world situations.

It's easy for the creators and the general public to balk at the impact fictional characters have on audiences, but research supports the idea that fiction affects real people.[25] Those who read comics and books, who watch movies and TV shows, and who play video games are affected by the fiction within, and it's an effect we carry with us long after we're finished with these stories, whether we realize it or not. Outside of our parents, fictional characters are often the first role models on which we base our behaviors. Creating complex characters audiences can identify with helps increase empathy for others, fosters a better understanding of ourselves, and, most obviously, makes for a good story.

The importance of having positive models we can identify with cannot be understated, whether these models are the adults in our lives or the superheroes in our fiction. As nascent human beings, we are particularly affected by the examples set by others; after all, much of our learning pattern comes from direct mimicry of what we see and hear. A father shaving in front of his child may find that child copying his motions using his or her toothbrush, or a parent who gets cut off in traffic may swear and then be surprised to hear his or her young child copy that swear word from the backseat. On the positive side, a child who observes his or her role models behaving with kindness and decency toward others and is encouraged by those role models to think deeply about such behaviors will probably go on to be a kinder, more decent person. Our brains learn from watching others, especially when we are young. Without altruistic examples such as Captain America to look up to, it seems that we are less likely to behave altruistically.

Inspiration

Captain America, regardless of who wears the mask, *inspires* people in a way that few other superheroes do. This character

THE LEGACY OF THE STARS AND STRIPES: CAP AS CULTURAL ADAPTATION

Modeling is an active process. Observers learn from behavioral models and then actively imitate those models, especially models valued by their culture.[26] Both prosocial and antisocial behaviors can be passed from person to person through imitation (*behavioral replication*).[27] Cultural evolution requires replication and adaptation.[28] During times when Steve Rogers goes missing, is believed dead, or quits being that superhero, the idea of Captain America carries on as a *cultural adaptation* through others who emulate him:

- **William Nasland**, President Truman's appointee as the new Captain America after Steve Rogers disappears toward the end of World War II.[29]
- **Jeffrey Mace**, Nasland's replacement upon his death.[30]
- **William Burnside**, the 1950s Captain America, initially heroic until his flawed Super-Soldier Serum turns him paranoid.[31]
- **Roscoe Simons**, a young man who assumes the title during Steve's brief stint as Nomad.[32]
- **Bob Russo and "Scar" Turpin**, each of whom becomes Cap for a single issue during Steve Rogers's hiatus.[33]
- **John Walker**, more commonly known as U.S. Agent or the Super-Patriot.[34]
- **Frank Castle**, the Punisher, who briefly becomes Captain America when Steve is believed dead after *Civil War*.[35]
- **James Buchanan "Bucky" Barnes,** Cap's former sidekick, to whom, following Steve's written request, Tony Stark hands over the title and shield.[36]
- **Dave Rickford**, Captain America for a short time until Steve Rogers rescues the somewhat incompetent Rickford from A.I.M.[37]
- **Sam Wilson**, previously known as the Falcon, who takes the title at Steve's request when the loss of his Super-Soldier formula effects ages Steve greatly.[38]

—A. L. & T. L.

has resonated with audiences for decades, all the way back to his origins as a World War II symbol of American heroism. Captain America has been referred to by fans as the ideal of old America; he's strong, kind, and certain in his morality, all qualities that resonate with those around him. Though Steve Rogers is a paragon of prosocial modeling in his own right, ultimately, it does not matter which man is under that mask so long as that man is a *good* man.

Comic Book References

Avengers #4 (1964). "Captan America Joins the Avengers!" Script: S. Lee. Art: J. Kirby & G. Roussos.

Captain America #155 (1972). "The Incredible Origin of the Other Captain America." Script: S. Englehart & S. Lee. Art: F. McLaughlin & J. Romita Jr.

Captain America #178 (1974). "If the Falcon Should Fall." Script: S. Englehart. Art: S. Buscema, V. Colleta, & P. Rachelson.

Captain America #179 (1974). "Slings and Arrows." Script: S. Englehart. Art: S. Buscema, V. Colleta, & P. Goldberg.

Captain America #181 (1974) "The Mark of Madness." Script: S. Englehart. Art: S. Buscema, V. Colleta, & L. Lessman.

Captain America #285 (1983). "Letting Go." Script: J. DeMatteis. Art: S. Buscema, K. Demulder, & B. Sharen.

Captain America #333 (1987). "The Replacement." Script: M. Gruenwald. Art: T. Morgan, D. Hunt, & K. Feduniewicz.

Captain America #5 (2005). "Out of Time." Script: E. Brubaker Art: S. Epting & M. Lark.

Captain America #25 (2007). "The Death of the Dream," part 1. Script: E. Brubaker. Art: S. Epting, & M. Perkins.

Captain America #33 (2008). "The Burden of Dreams," part 3. Script: E. Brubaker. Art: S. Epting & B. Guice.

Captain America #35 (2008). "The Man Who Bought America." Script: E. Brubaker. Art: S. Epting, & B. Guice.

Captain America #21 (2014). "The Iron Man, Part 5." Script: N. Klein & R. Remender. Art: N. Klein & D. White.

Captain America #22 (2014). "The Tomorrow Soldier," part 1. Script: R. Remender. Art: L. Loughridge, S. Immonen, C, Pacheco, M. Taibo, & D. White.

Captain America #25 (2014). "The Tomorrow Soldier: Conclusion." Script: R. Remender. Art: S. Immonen, C. Pacheco, M. Taibo, & D. White.

Punisher War Journal #7 (2007). "Blood and Sand." Script: M. Fraction. Art: A. Olivetti.

What If? #4 (1977). "What If the Invaders Had Stayed Together After World War Two?" Script: R. Thomas. Art: F. Robbins & F. Springer.

References

Bandura, A. (1986). *Social foundations of thoughts and action: A social cognitive theory.* New York, NY: Prentice Hall.

Bandura, A. (1989). A social cognitive theory of action. In J. P. Forgas & M. J. Innes (Eds.), *Recent advances in social psychology: An international perspective* (pp. 127–138). Amsterdam, Holland: Elsevier.

Bandura, A. (1997). *Self-efficacy: The exercise of control.* London, UK: Macmillan.

Berry, J. W., Worthington, E. J. Jr., Wade, N. G., van Oyen Witvliet, C., & Kiefer, R. P. (2005). Forgiveness, moral identity, and perceived justice in crime victims and their supporters. *Humboldt Journal of Social Relations, 29*(2), 136–162.

Boerner, K. (2003). To have and have not: Adaptive bereavement by transforming mental ties to the deceased. *Death Studies, 27*(3), 199–226.

Carlston, D. E., & Mae, L. (2007). Posing with the flag: Trait-specific effects of symbols on person perception. *Journal of Experimental Social Psychology, 43*(2), 241–248.

Dittmer, J. (2012). *Captain America and the nationalist superhero: Metaphors, narratives, and geopolitics.* Philadelphia, PA: Temple University Press.

Everett, J. A. C., Caviola, L., Kahane, G., Savulescu, J., & Faber, N. S. (2015). Doing good by doing nothing? The role of social norms in explaining default effects in social contexts. *European Journal of Social Psychology, 45*(2), 230–241.

Farsides, T., Pettman, D., & Tourle, L. (2013). Inspiring altruism: Reflecting on the personal relevance of emotionally evocative prosocial media characters. *Journal of Applied Social Psychology, 43*(11), 2251–2258.

Garcia, S. A., Clark, C., & Walfish, S. (1979). Student voluntarism in transition. *Journal of Community Psychology, 7*(1), 72–77.

Gibson, M. (2004). Melancholy objects. *Mortality, 9*(4), 285–299.

Hallam, E., & Hockey, J. (2001). *Death, memory, and material culture (materializing culture).* New York, NY: Berg.

Henrich, J., Boyd, R., & Richerson, P. J. (2008). Five misunderstandings about cultural evolution. *Human Nature, 19*(2), 119–137.

Oliner, S. P. (2005). Altruism, forgiveness, empathy, and intergroup apology. *Humboldt Journal of Social Relations, 29*(2), 8–39.

Papalia, D. E., & Martorell, G. (2015). *Experience human development* (13th ed.). New York, NY: McGraw-Hill.

Piaget, J., & Paul, K. (1926). *The language and thought of the child.* London, UK: Routledge.

Quartier, T. (2009). Personal symbols in Roman Catholic funerals in the Netherlands. *Mortality, 14*(2), 133–146.

Sanders, J. B., Seda, J. S., & Kardinal, C. G. (2013). Altruism: A coping mechanism for patients on clinical trials. *Clinical Journal of Oncology Nursing, 17*(5), 465–467.

Scobie, G. E. W., & Scobie, E. D. (2000). A comparison of forgiveness and pro-social development. *Early Child Development and Care, 160*(1), 33–45.

Simon, J., & Simon, J. (1990). *The comic book makers.* New York, NY: Vanguard.

Stroebe, M., Schut, H., & Boerner, K. (2010). Continuing bonds in adaptation to bereavement: Toward theoretical integration. *Clinical Psychology Review, 30*(2), 259–268.

Trumbore, D. (2012). *The Avengers assemble in these PSAs.* Collider: http://collider.com/the-avengers-psa/.

Wansink, B., Shimizu, M., & Camps, G. (2011). What would Batman eat? Priming children to make healthier food choices. *Pediatric Obesity, 7*(2), 121–123.

White, M. D. (2014). *The virtues of Captain America: Modern-day lessons on character from a World War II superhero*. Hoboken, NJ: Wiley-Blackwell.

White, R., & Carlson, S. (2015). What would Batman do? Self-distancing improves executive functioning in young children. *Developmental Science 6*(8), 1–8.

Notes

1. *Captain America: The Winter Soldier* (2014 motion picture).
2. Bandura (1997).
3. Quartier (2009).
4. Boerner (2003); Gibson (2004); Stroebe et al. (2010).
5. Simon & Simon (1990).
6. Bandura (1997).
7. Bandura (1997).
8. Farsides et al. (2013).
9. Dittmer (2012); White (2014).
10. Scobie & Scobie (2000).
11. Scobie & Scobie (2000).
12. Berry et al. (2005); Garcia et al. (1979); Oliner (2005).
13. *Captain America: The Winter Soldier* (2014 motion picture).
14. *Captain America: Civil War* (2016 motion picture).
15. Carlston & Mae (2007).
16. *Captain America* #25 (2007).
17. *Captain America* #33 (2008).
18. Sanders et al. (2013).
19. Bandura (1986).
20. Everett et al. (2015).
21. *Captain America: The Winter Soldier (*2014 motion picture).
22. Wansink et al. (2011).
23. White & Carlson (2015).
24. Piaget & Paul (1926).
25. Wansink et al. (2011); White & Carlson (2015).
26. Papalia & Martorell (2015).
27. Bandura (1989).
28. Henrich et al. (2008).
29. *What If?* #4 (1977).
30. *What If?* #4 (1977); Captain America #285 (1983).
31. *Captain America* #155 (1972).
32. *Captain America* #181 (1974).
33. *Captain America* #178–179 (1974).
34. *Captain America* #333 (1987).
35. *Punisher War Journal* #7 (2007).
36. *Captain America* #33 (2008).
37. *Captain America* #615.1 (2011).
38. *Captain America* #25 (2014).

A team's success or failure can hang on who leads it. Who should? The answer depends on who needs leading and when they need it. When heroes are larger than life, they may look to leaders who represent the most human qualities in them all.

CHAPTER TEN

LEADING THE EARTH'S MIGHTIEST HEROES

L A R A   T A Y L O R   K E S T E R

*"But we need a commander—someone who can
lead both teams, fuse us into one. I believe
that should be you, Captain America."*
—Superman (during the DC/Marvel crossover)[1]

*"A great person attracts great people and
knows how to hold them together."*
—writer Johann Goethe[2]

Just as each person has an individual personality, temperament, and motivation, each leader can have an individual *leadership style:* a measurably different way of leading a group.[3] Leaders can differ in whether they focus on the task or the people; the group or the individuals; whether the group serves the leader more than the leader serves the group; and whether the leader wields rigid control or shares it with group members.[4] The effectiveness of any leadership style can depend on the needs of the situation and the nature of the people involved.[5] Leaders of superhero teams who come together to save the world are no exception.

Captain America and Iron Man have very different ways of interacting with and leading the Avengers and other superheroes. Each has his own approach, but is either going about it in the best way? What works best when larger-than-life heroes with strong egos and diverse personalities fill the team? What qualities might lead someone to listen to the team's input rather than shut it out? Is there one "right" way to be a leader?

A Dichotomy of Styles

Historically, leadership has been viewed in a simplistic way, with two main styles of leaders. *Authoritarian leadership* is characterized by strong discipline, rigid rules, and an impersonal attitude toward subordinates.[6] Neither Steve nor Tony really fits this style unless under extreme stress. While Steve Rogers as Captain America is an example of a leader who can be rigid and structured, he is also willing to bend the rules at times to benefit others and is caring and compassionate toward the rest of his team. Tony seems to believe that he is superior to the rest of the Avengers and other superheroes, and his leadership style is less disciplined.

Another well-studied style, *democratic leadership*, focuses on creating job satisfaction by supporting team members, considering their needs, and consulting them on their areas of expertise. Cap exemplifies this style when he makes sure his team members are ready to take on challenges and encourages their input. However, a leader such as Tony Stark, who is more likely to disregard input he disagrees with or prefer to act on his own, may be less democratic.

Leadership Roles

Two main dimensions determine a leader's style of leadership: assertiveness and responsiveness.[7] *Assertiveness* refers to how directive or nondirective others consider the leader's behavior. Less assertive individuals are less likely to speak their minds in meetings and less likely to take control of situations. More assertive individuals are more likely to take charge and lead the way. *Responsiveness* refers to how emotionally controlled (or not) a leader's behaviors are. Individuals who are less responsive guard their feelings closely, whereas those who are more responsive show what they are feeling and react strongly to the emotions of those around them. Even though Steve may be caring and driven to do what his emotions tell him is right, he keeps his emotions in check when he is under pressure, whereas Tony reacts strongly to everything around him and more often leaps straight into action.

Degrees of assertiveness and responsiveness combine to form four distinct leadership styles (or roles) that leaders can adopt: the analyzer, the achiever, the relater, and the creator. The best leadership style may contain elements of all four roles.[8] Each role has its own strengths that it bring to a team (see table 10-1).

Analyzers are less responsive and less assertive. They tend to take in information systematically and gather all the facts before acting. Usually analyzers are well organized, possess great self-control, and refuse to compromise. Using Tony and Cap as examples, both borrow some traits from the analyzer category, such as Cap's caution and inquisitiveness when it comes to the inner workings of S.H.I.E.L.D. and Tony's focus and technical skills in a

TABLE 10-1. LEADERSHIP ROLES AND STRENGTHS			
Less responsive		More responsive	
Analyzer	Achiever	Relater	Creator
Less assertive	More assertive	Less assertive	More assertive
Cautious	Inquisitive	Active	Distinctive
Conservative	Logical	Competitive	Dominant
Contemplative	Serious	Confident	Efficient
Deliberative	Studious	Decisive	Independent
Focused	Technical	Disciplined	Strategic
Adaptive	Empathic	Communicative	Innovative
Connecting	Harmonizing	Enthusiastic	Involved
Consistent	Inclusive	Friendly	Persuasive
Developer	Loyal	Imaginative	Recognized
Diplomatic	Respectful	Impatient	Spontaneous

research and development lab, but neither neatly falls into this group. However, the Avengers sometimes have an analyzer in their midst (see the sidebar on Nick Fury on page 144).

Achievers are less responsive and more assertive. These leaders know what they want, can express those wants succinctly, and expect results. They are task-oriented and get to the point quickly. Achievers usually are perceived by others as confident, determined, decisive, and firm. Captain America falls into this role quite often, especially in a crisis. His military training has helped him learn to delegate tasks on the basis of his team's strengths and think on his feet.

Relaters are more responsive and less assertive. Leaders in this role are typically sympathetic to their followers and consider their needs when making decisions. Relaters often use empathy and understanding while problem-solving. Captain America is chosen to be the test subject for the serum because Dr. Erskine sees his compassion and caring for others.[9]

Creators are less responsive and less assertive. They typically take new, sometimes controversial approaches to leading a team. They tend to take risks in order to seize opportunities, believing that the ends justify the means. Creators are also very charming, inspiring, and persuasive. Tony appears as a textbook creator. He is innovative and inspirational and likes to be the center of attention. He also acts on impulse, which often puts him at odds with Captain America, who would prefer that Tony stop and think before he acts (such as when he created Ultron or when he creates the Vision).[10]

A good leader probably needs to be flexible and adaptive.[11] Leaders can borrow traits from roles other than the ones into which they primarily fall. Normally, a leader lacks the traits found in the role diagonally across from his or her role in the table.[12] The fact that Captain America embodies both the achiever and relater roles may be the reason he is fit to be the primary leader of the team. In a crisis or battle, he goes into achiever mode and takes charge. During times of calm and breaks from fighting, he checks in with his team to make sure they are okay and becomes more of a relater.

Even knowing that Cap is an exceptional leader, finding all four roles (analyzer, achiever, relater, and creator) in one person is virtually impossible. This is why leaders who exemplify such traits, such as Captain America, often need to partner with leaders who do not have them, such as Iron Man. Neither one alone can be everything his team needs, and that forces them to work together.

Motivating Heroes

Leaders need ways to motivate their teams to follow directions or complete objectives. Even heroes need motivation at times, especially when the situation looks dire. Without a leader to push the Avengers in the right direction, Loki would take over the world, Hydra would run S.H.I.E.L.D., or Earth would be annihilated during any of the global catastrophes superheroes frequently face.

There are two main styles of motivation that leaders can assume: transactional and transformational.[13] *Transactional motivation* uses bargaining, rewards, and punishment to gain control over the members of a team. Followers are compelled to act by external forces: the transactions. Leaders who use this style tend to be focused on the end result rather than helping followers become better at what they do.[14] When Spider-Man tries to leave Iron Man's side during the superheroes' Civil War, Tony uses transactional motivation. For example, he tries to blackmail Spider-Man and then resorts to threatening Spidey's aunt and wife to coerce him into staying; blackmail is acceptable to a leader who employs this style of leading and thinking.[15]

Transformational motivation, in contrast, changes the followers from within, motivating them to work toward common goals and seek rewards within themselves. This typically is seen as the more effective way of motivating followers, who are more personally invested in identifying with an organization beyond their own self-interest.[16] Leaders who use transformational motivation tend to be more supportive of their followers and act as guides to help facilitate personal growth. Even Tony Stark uses transformational motivation from time to time, for example, when he gets Bruce Banner to stew over "peace in our time" as a way to gain his help in creating Ultron.[17]

In reality, the best leaders tend to use both motivational styles adaptively.[18] Individuals respond differently to each type of motivation. Tony's attempt at blackmailing Spider-Man fails, and Spidey joins Captain America's Secret Avengers. Having two types of personalities who are opposed in many ways even though both take leadership roles makes the Avengers much more able to adapt to a variety of situations.

Self-Sacrifice

One aspect of being both a leader and a hero is self-sacrifice. *Self-sacrifice* is the willingness to incur personal costs or run the risk of those costs to serve the goals and mission of the group.[19] Leaders who engage in self-sacrificial behavior typically are considered by their followers to be more effective and charismatic and appear to value the team more than do leaders who do not engage in such behavior.

Not all sacrifices have to involve loss of life or running into danger, but in the world of villains and superheroes such as Captain America and Iron Man, many times they do. Captain America, no stranger to self-sacrifice, sneaks behind enemy lines by himself to save Bucky Barnes and the rest of the imprisoned soldiers[20] and often makes calls that could cause his death and save the world.[21] Even Tony Stark finds himself engaging in self-sacrifice when he flies a nuclear missile through a portal to space, believing that he will not make it back through.[22]

The difference between Cap's and Tony's sacrifices lies in the motivation behind them. Cap wants to save his friend because he feels loyal to him and cares about him. He crashes a plane into the ice to save New York because he believes in the greater good, the same reason he tells Maria Hill to blow up the Insight aircraft while he is still on board. Tony may want to save Earth when he flies the missile through the portal, but he also may be acting to prove a point to Captain America, who has criticized him for being unwilling to make necessary sacrifices.[23] Engaging in self-sacrifice for self-benefit is characteristic of a leader who uses a transactional motivation style. It may lead followers to view the leader as superficial or putting up a front.[24]

NICK FURY: A LEADER OF LEADERS

A well-balanced leadership team consists of all four basic leadership roles: achiever, relater, creator, and analyzer. Captain America (as more of an achiever and relator) and Iron Man (a creator) together illustrate three out of four of those styles and for the most part are able to handle the situations that come their way. However, without the fourth piece of the puzzle, a hole is left in their leadership, and that is a vulnerability they cannot afford. Enter the team's *analyzer*, Nick Fury, the Avengers' silent partner in some versions of their origin.[25]

Nick Fury embodies many of the strengths in the analyzer category. He holds his cards close to his chest, careful not to show his hand.[26] As a leader of a secret government organization with a host of spies at his command,[27] Fury could be considered very inquisitive and focused as well. His secrets allow him to surprise everyone and swoop in at the end to save the day, say, with a giant helicarrier.

Challengers

One role that may be found on a team is that of the *challenger*. Challengers are often perceived as a negative force on a team.[28] They express opposing views that challenge the team's current thinking or even the instructions of the leader. Although the general perception is that challenging the leader is a bad thing, in reality, it can cause the leader to think harder to find a better solution. While Cap is in the leadership position, Tony challenges him all the time, partly because that's what he does and partly to push Cap to think harder to find a solution that may be better. When Cap does not listen, Tony decides to take matters into his own hands and do what he wants to do anyway. Doing what he wants is not the same as doing what is best.

Another Dichotomy

"Soldiers trust each other. That's what makes it an army, not a bunch of guys running around shooting guns."
−Captain America[29]

Boiled down to its simplest form, leadership comes down to control versus trust. Authoritarian leaders are all about controlling their followers, while democratic leaders trust their followers to make positive decisions for the team. Achievers and creators tend to be about controlling the situation; analyzers and relaters sit back and trust the rest of the team to make the hard decisions. Transactional leaders want to be proactive in controlling the team's productivity; transformational leaders trust that the team will do what is best for themselves and others. Tony wants to control what the superheroes do and control the world to make it a better place, whereas Captain America trusts superheroes to support one another and feels that they will protect the world.[30]

No one way of leading is necessarily better than the others. Some tend to work better, but in reality, a good leader is able to adapt to the needs of the situation and the team. Captain America and Iron Man have different styles, although they are not that different from each other. They both can take charge in a crisis, they both want to help the world become a better place, and they both want the Avengers to succeed in their missions. Their methods may be different, but the goal is the same and each pushes the other to be a better as a leader, a hero, and a human being.

"Stories are the single most powerful tool in a leader's toolkit."

—psychologist Howard Gardner[31]

Comic Book References

Avengers/JLA #4 (2003). "The Brave and the Bold." Script: K. Busiek. Art: G. Perez.

Captain America #255 (1981). "The Living Legend." Script: R. Stern. Art: J. Byrne & J. Rubenstein.

Civil War #1–7 (2006–2007). Script: M. Millar. Art: S. McNiven, D. Vines, M. Hollowell, & C. Eliopoulos.

Original Sin #5 (2014). "The Secret History of Colonel Nicholas J. Fury." Script: J. Aaron. Art: M. Deodato.

Secret Avengers #5 (2010). "Secret Histories Epilogue: The Secret Life of Max Fury." Script: E. Brubaker. Art: D. Aja, M. Lark, S. Gaudiano, & J. Villarrubia.

Strange Tales #135 (1965). "Nick Fury, Agent of S.H.I.E.L.D.: The Man for the Job." Script: S. Lee. Art: J. Kirby.

The Ultimates #2 (2002). "Big." Script: M. Millar. Art: B. Hitch & A. Currie.

References

Bucic, T., Robinson, L., & Ramburuth, P. (2010). Effects of leadership style on team learning. *Journal of Workplace Learning, 22*(4), 228–248.

Cerni, T., Curtis, G. J., & Colmar, S. H. (2014). Cognitive-experiential leadership model: How leaders' information-processing systems can influence leadership styles, influencing tactics, conflict management, and organizational outcomes. *Journal of Leadership Studies, 8*(3), 26–39.

Darling, J., & Heller, V. (2012). Effective organizational consulting across cultural boundaries: A case focusing on leadership styles and team-building. *Organization Development Journal, 30*(4), 54–72.

De Vries, R. E., Bakker-Pieper, A., & Oostenveld, W. (2010). Leadership = communication? The relations of leaders' communication styles with leadership styles, knowledge sharing and leadership outcomes. *Journal of Business and Psychology, 25*(3), 367–380.

Fiedler, F. E. (1987, September). When to lead, when to stand back. *Psychology Today,* pp. 26–27.

Getha-Taylor, H., Silvia, C., & Simmerman, S. (2014). Individuality, integration: Leadership styles in team collaboration. *The Public Manager, 43*(2), 38–43.

Goethe, J. (1790) *Torquato Tasso,* act I, scene I. Ed. Des Voeux, C. Weimar, Germany

Hogan, R., Curphy, C. J., & Hogan, J. (1994). What we know about leadership: Effectiveness and personality. *American Psychologist, 49*(6), 493-504.

Lewin, K., Lippitt, R., & White, R. K. (1939). Patterns of aggressive behavior in experimentally created "social climates." *Journal of Social Psychology*, 10, 271–299.

Odoardi, C., Montani, F., Boudrias, J., & Battistelli, A. (2015). Linking managerial practices and leadership style to innovative work behavior: The role of group and psychological processes. *Leadership and Organization Development Journal*, *36*(5), 545–569.

Pratt, S., & Eitzen, D. (1989). Contrasting leadership styles and organizational-effectiveness—the case of athletic teams. *Social Science Quarterly*, *70*(2), 311–322.

Rossetti, L. (2013). Storytelling for talent development. In T. Wall & J. Knights (Eds.), *Leadership assessment for talent development* (pp. 197–218). London, UK: Kogan Page.

Ruggieri, S., & Abbate, C. S. (2013). Leadership style, self-sacrifice, and team identification. *Social Behavior and Personality: An International Journal*, *41*(7), 1171–1178.

Zorn, T. E., & Violanti, M. T. (1993). Measuring leadership style: A review of leadership style instruments for classroom use. *Communication Education, 42*(1), 70–78.

Notes

1. *Avengers/JLA* #4 (2003).
2. Goethe (1790).
3. Zorn (1993).
4. Fiedler (1987); Hogan et al. (1994); Lewin et al. (1939).
5. Odoardi et al. (2015).
6. Pratt & Eitzen (1989).
7. Darling & Heller (2012).
8. Darling & Heller (2012).
9. *Captain America* #255 (1981); *Captain America: The First Avenger* (2011 motion picture).
10. *The Avengers: Age of Ultron* (2015 motion picture).
11. Darling & Heller (2012); de Vries et al. (2010); Getha-Taylor et al. (2014).
12. Darling & Heller (2012).
13. Cerni et al. (2014).
14. Ruggieri & Abbate (2013).
15. *Civil War* #5 (2007).
16. Ruggieri & Abbate (2013).
17. *Avengers: Age of Ultron* (2015 motion picture).
18. Bucic et al. (2010).
19. Ruggieri & Abbate.
20. *Captain America: The First Avenger* (2011 motion picture).
21. *Captain America: The First Avenger* (2011); *Captain America: The Winter Soldier* (2014 motion picture).
22. *The Avengers* (2012 motion picture).
23. *The Avengers: Age of Ultron* (2015 motion picture).
24. Ruggieri & Abbate (2013).
25. *The Avengers* (2012 motion picture); *The Ultimates* #2 (2002).
26. e.g., *The Avengers* (2012 motion picture); *Original Sin* #5 (2014).
27. *Strange Tales* #135 (1965).
28. Getha-Taylor et al. (2014).
29. *Captain America: The Winter Soldier* (2014 motion picture).
30. *Civil War* #1–7 (2006–2007).
31. Rosetti (2013).

SUPEREGO

TRAVIS LANGLEY

During the preschool years, children's sense of morality expands beyond simply avoiding punishment and seeking rewards as they begin adding basic concepts of right and wrong. In their related theories on cognitive and moral development, psychologists Jean Piaget[1] and Lawrence Kohlberg[2] said that this happens because of children's growing capacity for complex thought. Erik Erikson attributed it to the fact that they are beginning to care what others think of them, seeking *social approval*. Sigmund Freud[3] speculated that children develop morals to protect their genitals—conscience as codpiece. Regardless of their differing views on why morals emerge, their observations fairly well match with regard to when morals emerge.

For example, a person like the character Steve Rogers may have a strong sense of morality throughout his lifetime, whereas someone like Tony Stark must make a concerted effort to look out for others even after a trauma-generated epiphany leads him to reevaluate his priorities.[4] From a psychodynamic point of view, Steve develops the stronger *superego*, the part of personality that includes his powerful conscience. Tony learns moral concepts in childhood as well but assigns them less importance. For Steve, morality is an ingrained, automatic part of who he is as a human being, his psychological *baseline*.

According to Freud, children in the third psychosexual stage, the *phallic stage*, develop the superego through *identification* with their fathers or the paternal figures in their lives. "The installation of the super-ego can be described as a successful instance of identification with the parental agency," Freud wrote.[5] Children supposedly—repeat, *supposedly*—do this to resolve their *Oedipus conflict* (attraction to the opposite-sex parent or parental figure and related feelings of rivalry with the same-sex one). Because false memories of his early life (*pseudomemories*) have been implanted in him,[6] it's hard to know what kind of relationship Steve has with his parents during his childhood. If a boy has a healthy relationship with his father, Freud might interpret his later strong sense of morality as a successful identification with his father, but a bad relationship[7] would allow for a Freudian suggestion that he acts morally and assertively as a way of defying his father. Freud said that little boys have *castration anxiety*, worrying that their fathers will cut off the boys' genitals, and that little girls experience *penis envy*, envying the males for having a complete anatomy as if nature itself has castrated girls. Even though many sources credit Freud for suggesting that girls experience a comparable *Electra complex* (developing the superego through identification with their mothers in order to resolve feelings of rivalry with their fathers), they are wrong. It was the psychiatrist Carl Jung[8] who suggested that possibility and coined the term, an idea that Freud explicitly rejected.[9] As Freud saw it, each little boy grows his superego to keep his penis from getting cut off and each little girl does so to make up for not having one.

From a psychodynamic perspective, Steve's stronger, steadier scruples and Tony's lingering need to make peace with his father's memory could suggest that Steve more successfully resolved emotional issues from before age seven. Freud and Erikson would agree on that up to a point, but whereas Freud's psychosexual interpretation would attribute it to childhood Oedipal issues, Erikson's psychosocial view would describe their outcomes in terms of the *initiative vs. guilt* stage. Steve and Tony, who both are able to take initiative, show many signs of having received good parenting, although Tony's parenting appears to have been less consistent.[10] Although both also feel guilt, Steve lets himself face feelings of guilt over events such as the death of Bucky[11] and copes with guilt in healthier ways. Because Tony is more prone than Steve to avoid facing the guilt that he does feel, he has less experience learning and using healthy coping behaviors. Tony therefore will go to more extreme lengths to manage feelings of guilt or anxiety, obviously including his drinking but also including some of his more egotistical moments.

In Freudian terminology, a *narcissistic wound* occurs when circumstances threaten a narcissist's sense of self-worth or self-esteem. For a narcissist who feels a strong need for power over his or her world, failure feels likely to incur scorn as if an echo of early fear of parental rejection. Each time Tony Stark launches into a period of excessive drinking, extreme events have threatened his image and shaken his sense of control over his life. Regardless of whether they agree with its Oedipal origin, numerous researchers have worked to expand our understanding of the narcissistic wound and the rage that may be associated with it.

Freud saw *narcissism* as sexual preoccupation with oneself, so that an egotistical person must be sexually focused on himself or herself—erotically preoccupied with the one lover each most wants to satisfy, the self.[12] During Tony's frequent sexual exploits, he shows signs of selfishness, such as dismissing his sex partners afterward or failing to remember who a number of them are.[13] When someone with such an advanced memory has difficulty remembering sexual partners' names, it suggests that their individual identities mattered little to him.[14] Freud saw narcissism as a manifestation of *fixation* (being emotionally stuck) in the phallic stage. Numerous individuals whose dealings with Tony Stark have not gone to their liking certainly might accuse him of having a phallic personality, although perhaps in coarser language.

The superego's demands oppose the id's. The ego, still learning how best to comfort the id, must now deny that impulsive, instinctive part of personality sometimes to satisfy the demanding superego. Whereas Tony Stark more often satisfies his id, Steve Rogers frequently *sublimates* that energy and directs it into other activities. For example, instead of dating much, he dedicates himself to his mission and throws himself into his work. Instead of letting the Black Widow fix him up on a date with someone, Cap punches agents of HYDRA.[15] He does not fully neglect that side of his life, though, because between lengthy spells of singlehood, he has a couple of long-term girlfriends at different times over the years.[16] Even though his superego is a powerful part of him, it does not rule him entirely.

Because Freud felt that personality is largely formed by age five or six and unlikely to change much thereafter (despite empirical evidence that personality does keep changing[17]), a Freudian view might suggest that those earliest years set the stage for Captain America and Iron Man to proceed on their different paths to heroism and on the road to their Civil War.

Comic Book References

The Avengers #4 (1964). "Captain America Joins the Avengers!" Script: S. Lee. Art: J. Kirby & G. Roussos.

Captain America #247 (1980). "By the Dawn's Early Light!" Script: R. Stern & J. Byrne. Art: J. Byrne & J. Rubenstein.

Captain America #294 (1984, June). "The Measure of a Man." Script: J. M. DeMatteis. Art: P. Neary & J. Rubinstein.

Captain America #30 (2007, November). "The Death of the Dream," part 6. Script: E. Brubaker. Art: S. Epting & M. Perkins.

Captain America #1 (2013). "Castaway in Dimension Z," part 1. Script: R. Remender. Art: J. Romita Jr. & K. Janson.

Iron Man #28 (1970). "The Controller Lives!" Script: A. Goodwin. Art: D. Heck & J. Craig.

Tales of Suspense #39 (1963). "Iron Man!" Script: S. Lee. Art: J. Kirby & D. Heck.

Other References

Freud, S. (1909). Analysis of a phobia in a 5-year-old boy. In *Jahrbuch für psychoanalytische under psychopathologische Forshugen*, Bd. 1. Reprinted in *The sexual enlightenment of childen* (1963). New York, NY: Collier.

Freud, S. (1914/1963). On narcissism. In P. Rieff (Ed.), *General psychological theory* (pp. 56–82). New York, NY: Collier.

Freud, S. (1920/2001). Psychogenesis of a case of homosexuality in a woman. In J. Strachey (Ed. & Trans.), *The standard edition of the complete works of Sigmund Freud*, Vol. XVIII (pp. 147–172). London, UK: Vintage.

Freud, S. (1933). New introductory lectures on psycho-analysis. In *The standard edition of the complete psychological works of Sigmund Freud*, vol. XXII (pp.1–182). London, UK: Hogarth.

Freud, S. (1940). An outline of psychoanalysis. In *Standard edition of the complete works of Sigmund Freud* (vol. 23, pp. 141–207). London, UK: Hogarth.

Jung, C. G. (1913). The theory of psychoanalysis. *Psychoanalytic Review*, *1*(1), 1–40.

Kagan, J., Kearsley, R., & Zelazo, P. (1978). *Infancy*. Cambridge, MA: Harvard University Press.

Kohlberg, L. (1981). *Essays on moral development*. San Francisco, CA: Harper & Row.

Klimstra, T. A., Bleidorn, W., Adendorpf, J. B., van Aken, M. A. G., & Denissen, J. J. A. (2013). Correlated change of Big Five personality traits across the lifespan: A search for determinants. *Journal of Research in Personality*, *47*(6), 768–777.

Magee, C. A., Heaven, P. C. L., & Miller, L. M. (2013). Personality change predicts self-reported mental and physical health. *Journal of Personality*, *81*(3), 324–334.

Piaget, J. (1932). *The moral judgment of the child*. New York, NY: Harcourt Brace Jovanovich.

Notes

1. Kohlberg (1981); Piaget (1932).
2. Kohlberg (1981).
3. Freud (1909, 1940).
4. *Tales of Suspense* #39.

5. Freud (1933), p. 80.
6. *Captain America* #247 (1980).
7. Freud (1909, 1940).
8. Jung (1913).
9. Freud (1920/2001).
10. *Iron Man* #28 (1970).
11. *The Avengers* #4 (1964).
12. Freud (1914/1963).
13. e.g., *Iron Man* (2008 motion picture); *Iron Man 2* (2010 motion picture).
14. *Iron Man*; *Iron Man 2* (2008, 2010 motion pictures).
15. *Captain America: The Winter Soldier* (2013 motion picture).
16. *Captain America* #294 (1984); #30 (2007).
17. e. g., Kagan et al (1978); Klimstra et al. (2013); Magee et al. (2013).

STRUGGLE

"I can create a world without war. . . . Without hate or jealousy. But then it wouldn't be the world we live in. Nothing would be learned, nothing would be gained. We wouldn't advance as a species."
—Tony Stark[1]

"If there is no struggle, there is no progress."
—social reformer and former slave Frederick Douglass[2]

Life is a struggle.

Struggle—having to make a great effort to achieve a goal, whether great or small—can tear us down or build us up. Struggle strengthens muscles, sharpens wit, and makes stories more intriguing. We value our achievements or find greater meaning in them when we have suffered more to reach them.[3] The poor kid from Brooklyn who grows up struggling to stand up to others and the rich kid who eventually gets held captive in a cave both choose to become bigger, stronger, and larger than life and then dedicate their new strengths to fighting for others. Their struggles help them grow and mature. Ours can, too.

Through this "vs." book, we have compared and contrasted two men in a number of ways. For all their differences in background (poor and weak; rich and healthy) and maybe motives (patriotism and empathy; narcissism and guilt), their similarities in areas such as assertiveness and their decisions to do what's right bring them together most of the time. Differences draw attention, but psychologists have shown repeatedly that similarities are greater predictors of when people will like each other and work well together,[4] especially similarities in attitudes.[5] It is a difference in *attitude* (a view on whether something is favorable or unfavorable[6]) that eventually pits them and other heroes against one another in a conflict that appears to be *zero-sum*: One side loses; the other side wins. When there appears to be no room for negotiation to find middle ground, a destructive struggle may never end.[7]

The superheroes' Civil War ends when Captain America, on the verge of defeating Iron Man, instead surrenders because their destructive conflict needs to end.[8] Seeing that winning in the field would require losing philosophically, he accepts imprisonment for the sake of the greater good and soon is assassinated by a sniper (or so it seems) on his way to court.[9] "It's a hell of a time for him to go," creator Joe Simon said at age 93. "We really need him now."[10] Simon lived to see the character's return,[11] though, and then the theatrical success of the film *Captain America: The First Avenger* as well.[12] His observation reflects his awareness of his creation's symbolic importance, the inspirational and motivation value people can gain from a hero regardless of whether that hero was born in a hospital or on a page.

When psychologist Erich Fromm referred to the conflict between freedom and security as the most basic human dilemma, he never suggested that either side could win conclusively over the other because we need both. Without both chaos and order, we are stagnant. The human struggle continues, and that is part of being alive. Superheroes never fully vanquish supervillains, police never remove all criminals from the streets, and doctors never cure all diseases, but the effort along the way accomplishes much good and lets people learn much more about themselves and others who share the same world.

Struggle is life.

"The most beautiful people we have known are those who have known defeat, known suffering, known struggle, known loss, and have found their way out of the depths."
—psychiatrist Elisabeth Kübler-Ross[13]

"One day in retrospect the years of struggle will strike you as the most beautiful."
—psychoanalyst Sigmund Freud[14]

Comic Book References

The Amazing Spider-Man #67 (1968). "To Squash a Spider!" Script: S. Lee. Art: J. Romita & J. Mooney.

The Amazing Spider-Man #532–537 (2006–2007). "The War at Home." Script: J. M. Straczynski. Art: R. Garney & B. Reinhold.

Avengers #12 (2011). "Who Will Wield the Gauntlet?" Script: B. M. Bendis. Art: J. Romita Jr. & K. Janson.

Captain America #25 (2007). "The Death of the Dream." Script: E. Brubaker. Art: S. Epting.

Captain America: Reborn #1–7 (2009–2010). Script: E. Brubaker. Art: B. Hitch & B. Guice.

Civil War #1–7 (2006–2007). Script: M. Millar. Art: S. McNiven, D. Vines, M. Hollowell, & C. Eliopoulos.

Civil War #7 (2007). Script: M. Millar. Art: S. McNiven.

Other References

Byrne, D. (1971). *The attraction paradigm*. New York, NY: Academic Press.

Cole, T., & Teboul, J. C. B. (2004). Non-zero-sum collaboration, reciprocity, and the preference for similarity: Developing an adaptive model of close relational functioning. *Personal Relationships, 11*(2), 135–160.

Douglass, F. (1857). *Two speeches by Frederick Douglass*. Rochester, NY: Dewey.

Festinger, L. (1961). The psychological effects of insufficient rewards. *American Psychologist, 16*(1), 1–11.

Freud, E. L. (1960/1992). *Letters of Sigmund Freud*. Mineola, NY: Dover.

Kübler-Ross, E. (1975). *Death: The final stage of growth*. New York, NY: Touchstone.

Maio, G. R., & Haddock, G. (2010). *The psychology of attitudes and attitude change*. London, UK: Sage.

Osbeck, L. M., Moghaddam, F. M., & Perreault, S. (1996). Similarity and attraction among majority and minority groups in a multicultural context. *International Journal of Intercultural Relations, 20*(1), 1–10.

Sacks, E. (2007, March 9). *Captain America killed!* New York Daily News: http://www.nydaily news.com/entertainment/music-arts/captain-america-killed-article-1.217626.

Shannon, H. M. (2014, March 5). *Captain America lives on: Remembering Joe Simon*. Bleeding Cool: http://www.bleedingcool.com/2014/03/05/captain-america-lives -on-remembering-joe-simon/.

Wilkins, C. L., Wellman, J. D., Babbitt, L. G., Toosi, N. R., & Schad, K. D. (2015). You can win but I can't lose: Bias against high-status groups increases their zero-sum beliefs about discrimination. *Journal of Experimental Social Psychology, 57*(1), 1–14.

Notes

1. *Avengers* 12 (2011).
2. Douglass (1957).
3. Festinger (1961).
4. Osbeck et al. (1996).
5. Byrne (1971);
6. Maio & Haddock (2010).
7. Cole & Teboul (2004); Wilkins et al. (2015).
8. *Civil War* #7 (2007).
9. *Captain America* #25 (2007).
10. Sacks (2007).
11. *Captain America: Reborn* #1–7 (2006–2007).
12. Shannon (2014).
13. Kübler-Ross (1975), p. 96.
14. Letter to C. G. Jung, published by E. L. Freud (1960/1992), p. 258.

ABOUT THE EDITOR

 Travis Langley, PhD, editor of *The Walking Dead Psychology: Psych of the Living Dead,* *Star Wars Psychology: Dark Side of the Mind,* and *Captain America vs. Iron Man: Freedom, Security, Psychology,* is a psychology professor who teaches courses on crime, media, and mental illness at Henderson State University. He received a bachelor's degree from Hendrix College and graduate degrees in psychology from Tulane University in New Orleans. Dr. Langley regularly speaks on media and heroism at conventions and universities. *Necessary Evil: Super-Villains of DC Comics* and other films have featured him as an expert interviewee, and the documentary *Legends of the Knight* spotlighted the way he uses fiction to teach real psychology. He authored the acclaimed book *Batman and Psychology: A Dark and Stormy Knight. Psychology Today* carries his blog "Beyond Heroes and Villains."

Follow him as @Superherologist on Twitter, where he ranks among the ten most popular psychologists. You can also keep up with Travis and the book's superteam of contributors at Facebook.com/ThePsychGeeks.

On his office wall: original illustrations of Iron Man playing golf by Bob Layton, whom some call the definitive Iron Man artist, and Captain America by Allen Bellman, last of the early Timely Comics artists.

ABOUT THE CONTRIBUTORS

 Jenna Busch is a journalist and the founder of Legion of Leia, a website to promote and support women in fandom. She co-hosted "Cocktails with Stan" with Spider-Man co-creator and comic book legend Stan Lee and has appeared in the film *She Makes Comics*, as a guest on *Attack of the Show*, and on NPR, Al Jazeera American, and multiple episodes *of Tabletop with Wil Wheaton*. She's a comic book author, co-host of *Most Craved*, and weekly columnist for Metro. Busch has co-authored chapters in *Star Wars Psychology*, *Game of Thrones Psychology*, and *Star Trek Psychology*. Her work has appeared all over the Web, and she is one of this volume's assistant editors. You can reach her on Twitter at @JennaBusch.

 **Josué Cardona** is a licensed clinical psychotherapist and entrepreneur. He is a technology, language, and culture expert, with an emphasis on geek culture. He speaks frequently at popular culture and professional conventions and is the founder of GeekTherapy.com. His published works include a chapter in *The Walking Dead Psychology: Psych of the Living Dead*. Find him on Twitter as @JosueACardona.

 Tommy Cash graduated from Henderson State University, a school he chose partly because of its curriculum involving comic books. This allowed him to call reading an issue of *Fantastic Four* (which he had been reading anyway) "homework."

Comics have been part of his life since his mother bought him, at age three, a *Tom and Jerry* comic book at a used book store. He has spoken on the psychology and cultural significance of superheroes at the Comics Arts Conference and other scholarly events. His published works include entries in *Icons of the American Comic Book: From Captain America to Wonder Woman* (ABC-CLIO). He works with adults who have developmental disabilities.

J. Scott Jordan, PhD, has held fellowships at the University of Ulm in Germany, the Max Planck Institute for Psychological Research in Munich, and the Center for Interdisciplinary Research at the University of Bielefeld in Germany. He has published over 70 papers, co-edited 9 books and journal special issues, and given more than 60 invited talks. His research focuses on the relationship between consciousness, action, self, and identity.

Lara Taylor Kester, MA, holds a degree in counseling psychology as well as a certificate in traumatology and treatment from Holy Names University. A registered marriage and family therapy intern who works with at-risk and foster youth in the San Francisco Bay Area, she created TherapeuticCode.com and serves as a contributing editor at GeekTherapy.com. She has authored chapters in *The Walking Dead Psychology* and *Game of Thrones Psychology*.

Alan "Sizzler" Kistler is a screenwriter and actor. His published books include the *New York Times* bestseller *Doctor Who: A History* (Lyons). As a pop culture historian focusing on science fiction and superheroes, he has contributed to news sites such as Polygon.com, Wired.com, TheMarySue.com, ComicBookResources.com, and MTV Splashpage. He created and hosts the podcast *Crazy Sexy Geeks*, has co-authored chapters in *The Walking Dead Psychology* and *Star Trek Psychology*, and tweets as @SizzlerKistler.

Alex Langley, MS, allegedly has a borderline nuclear passion for writing. He has authored *The Geek Handbook* series of books on geek culture (Krause), successfully crowdsourced his graphic novel *Kill the Freshman*, and contributed a chapter to *Star Wars Psychology: Dark Side of the Mind*. He writes about retro and modern gaming for Arcade Sushi, edits content for geekgirl/web celebrity Katrina Hill at ActionFlickChick.com, and can be found online as @RocketLlama on Twitter.

Martin Lloyd, PhD, LP, received his doctorate in clinical psychology from the University of Minnesota. He has worked in various prisons and high-security hospitals, including the United States Medical Center for Federal Prisoners and Patton State Hospital. He practices as a forensic psychologist in Minnesota and occasionally teaches forensic psychology at Gustavus Adolphus College. At age 10, he read his first superhero comic book, *Captain America* #350 by Mark Gruenwald and Kieron Dwyer, beginning a lifelong love of the superhero genre.

Patrick O'Connor, PsyD, is the creator of Comicspedia, an online tool that assists therapists in using comic books in therapy. He teaches at the Chicago School of Professional Psychology, where he debuted the course "Geek Culture in Therapy," in which students discover how geek culture plays a role in our understanding of ourselves and others and how geek culture artifacts are the vehicles through which we develop this understanding.

Billy San Juan, PsyD, received his doctorate in 2014 and is a post-doctoral intern in San Diego, CA. He has contributed chapters to *The Walking Dead Psychology, Star Wars Psychology*, and *Star Trek Psychology*. His public appearances have included panels at conventions such as San Diego Comic-Con International and Stan Lee's Comikaze Expo. He is a Level 1 *Magic: The Gathering* judge and has written articles for the community on topics such as customer service and burnout.

Janina Scarlet, PhD, is a licensed clinical psychologist, Alliant International University faculty member, and full-time geek. She uses Superhero Therapy to help patients with anxiety, depression, chronic pain, and PTSD at the Center for Stress and Anxiety Management and Sharp Memorial Hospital. Dr. Scarlet authored the book *Superhero Therapy* (Little, Brown) and has authored chapters in the Sterling Publishing works *The Walking Dead Psychology*, *Star Wars Psychology*, *Game of Thrones Psychology*, and *Star Trek Psychology*. She can be reached at her website superhero-therapy.com and on Twitter @shadowquill.

Eric D. Wesselmann, PhD, an assistant professor of psychology at Illinois State University, earned his doctorate in social psychology in 2011 from Purdue University. He teaches undergraduate and graduate courses on social psychology, statistics, research, and the psychology of film. His published research has explored ostracism, stigma, and religion/spirituality. He is a consulting editor for *The Journal of Social Psychology* and has been a comic book fan since grade school. When not at work, he and his spouse train their three little superheroes at home to be the best heroes they can be.

 **Mara Wood,** PhD, is a school psychology specialist in the public school system. Her research focus is the educational application of comic books and their therapeutic use with children and adolescents. She has presented research on transportation and identification with comic book characters at the Comics Arts Conference. She is a regular contributor to Talking Comics, co-hosts "The Missfits" and "Talking Shojo" podcasts, and writes about psychology, comics, books, and *Dungeons & Dragons* on her blog at marawoodblog.com. Dr. Wood is one of this volume's assistant editors. Find her on twitter as @MegaMaraMon.

 **E. Paul Zehr,** PhD, is a professor, author, and martial artist at the University of Victoria, where he teaches in the neuroscience, kinesiology, and Island Medical programs. His pop-sci books include *Becoming Batman* (2008), *Inventing Iron Man* (2011), *Project Superhero* (2014), and *Something Superhuman* (2016). *Maxim*, CNN, NPR, and others have interviewed him for his diverse expertise. Paul writes for *Psychology Today*, *Scientific American*, *Discover*, and *Digital Journal*.

SPECIAL CONTRIBUTOR

**Stan Lee** is known to millions as the man whose Super Heroes propelled Marvel to its preeminent position in the comic book industry. His co-creations include Spider-Man™*, the Avengers ™, X-Men™, Iron Man™, the Incredible Hulk™, and the Fantastic Four™, as well as hundreds of others. He introduced Spider-Man™ as a syndicated newspaper strip that became the most successful of all syndicated adventure strips and has appeared in more than 500 newspapers worldwide. Stan currently remains Chairman Emeritus of Marvel, as well as a member of the Editorial Board of Marvel Comics.

Stan is currently the Chairman & Chief Creative Officer of POW! Entertainment, a multimedia entertainment company based in Beverly Hills, CA, which he founded with production partner Gill Champion & Arthur Lieberman. POW! has debuted several titles in the publishing sphere, including Stan's graphic memoir *Amazing Fantastic Incredible* with Simon & Schuster; the first two books of the *Zodiac* trilogy with Disney Publishing; *Soldier Zero*, *Traveler*, and *Starborn* with Boom Comics; *Romeo and Juliet: The War* with 1821 Comics; and *Stan Lee and the Mighty 7* with Archie Comics and Genius Brands International. Additionally, *Stan Lee and the Mighty 7* premiered as an animated TV movie broadcast on the Hub. Stan has been involved in developing feature film projects, including *Annihilator*, *Prodigal*, and *Replicator & Antilight*, as well as TV projects including *Stan Lee's Lucky Man* and *Hellana*. He released his first-ever Indian superhero, *Chakra: The Invincible*, which debuted on Cartoon Network in India and can be watched on the Rovio ToonsTV app, and is currently working on a number of potential superhero franchises.

*All trademarks indicated above are owned by Marvel Entertainment, LLC.

PICTURE CREDITS

INDEX

(*continued*)